Break Free

From Your Sexual Past

A Study of Freedom, Forgiveness, Healing and Hope

Barbara Wilson

BREAK FREE FROM YOUR SEXUAL PAST

Published by Lightning Source

1246 Heil Quaker Blvd.
La Vergne, TN USA 37086
www.lightningsource.com

ISBN ~ 13:9780615300658

Cover Design by Matthew Wright

Interior Design and typeset by Matthew Wright

Unless otherwise stated, Scripture quotations are from:

The Holy Bible, New International Version

Library of Congress Cataloging-in-Publication Data

ACKNOWLEDGEMENTS

Every attempt has been made to credit the sources of copyrighted material used in this book. If any such acknowledgment has been inadvertently omitted or miscredited, receipt of such information would be appreciated.

For Information:

Barbara Wilson
P.O. Box 2092
Granite Bay, Ca. 95746
www.barbarawilson.org

Wilson, Barbara J. Break Free From Your Sexual Past

Printed in the United States of America

BREAK FREE FROM YOUR SEXUAL PAST

CONTENTS

ENDORSEMENTS

Here are comments from some of the women who've gone through this study:

"I was always trying to fill the emptiness in my heart. Through this study I found the cause of the emptiness and was able to allow God to fill my heart. My life/marriage will never be the same."

"This study not only changed my life it brought me back into the arms of my husband and to God where I belong."

"This study made me open my eyes to my past sexual experiences and how they affected the choices I made in my life."

"This study has completely renewed my relationship with the Lord. I came into the study wanting a better more fulfilling sex life and came out with a hunger for the Lord again! I wasn't sure my marriage was going to work and this study has given me the tools and hope to overcome the emotional and spiritual obstacles that have been keeping me from being close to my husband. I now have God 's perspective on sex and His Word has healed me in more areas of my life than just sex! He is still healing me and I feel like I am on an adventure."

"I want to tell you what a life changing experience it was going through the bible study. I have a new freedom, a new confidence, increased faith, and just an overall sense of well being. It brought me to a place of being okay with me, something I have struggled with all of my life."

"Through this study the Lord started me on a journey of recovery and forgiveness. I thought the whole study would be focused on my horrible choices, and the shame that I carried with them. But the Lord in His grace and goodness showed me He didn't see my mistakes. He saw my pain and He wanted to take it from me as He had already paid the price for them.

Eventually, I was able to forgive myself and the men involved in my past. I was also able, for the first time in my life pray for the man who sexually abused me as a small child. This study allowed me to let go of the shame of my past and begin to heal the wounded areas of my life. It is a journey I am still on. I so desperately wanted freedom in my life and when I called out to the Lord He opened the doors. This study is a gift from God."

"This bible study has revolutionized our sex life opening up new levels of intimacy in not just a physical way but a spiritual and emotional way as well. It has ignited new passion to know one another and walk the life journey together. Fasten your seat belts, this bible study will change you and your marriage forever."

"My marriage and life is more blessed than I could have ever imaged. My husband and I have an incredible marriage, that includes good communication, trust, love and now... thanks to your bible study, one heck of a sex life."

This book is dedicated to:

The One who's grace is amazing.

Whose love is unending.

Whose forgiveness and mercy has set me free.

To the Source of all I am, all I have, and all I'm becoming.

To Jesus Christ, my Savior, Lord and dearest Friend.

INTRODUCTION

This isn't like any Bible Study you've ever experienced. Everything about it is different. Besides developing a deeper intimacy with God, this study will walk you through a grieving process for your sexual past, whether from your own choices or other's choices forced on you. Through this life-changing study God will heal the wounds you've accumulated because of your sexual past, help you grieve the losses you've experienced, sever the ungodly sexual soul ties you've created and replace the lies you've ingrained with His truth.

Like many of the women who've taken this journey before, you may be feeling excited and scared at the same time. You're excited because you know God has called you to this place and you have a sense of anticipation and hope of what He's going to do. But you may also be scared of what's to come, afraid that although God's done it for others, He can't or won't do it for you. Don't be discouraged. You're not alone in how you feel. I've been there too. Trust in that hope you're feeling because it's from God, whereas your fear is not. I'm not saying it's going to be easy--at first it may be painful--but this will be good pain, the kind that will forever heal the hurt you've been living with.

Before you start Chapter One, fill out the assessment forms at the beginning of the study. These will give you an accurate picture of where you are right now and help you acknowledge your wounds. If you're doing this in a group, you may be asked to share these with your leaders during an intake interview. Keep these forms to compare with the same ones you'll complete in Chapter Twelve of this study. They will provide measurable proof of the incredible healing God will do in your life.

This study is based on my book, *The Invisible Bond; How to break free from your sexual past,* published by Multnomah, 2006. You'll notice that I refer to this book and ask you to read certain sections to further your understanding of some passages, as well as quote from the book throughout the study. I advise you to get a copy of this book to help you as you go through this study. You can order it from any bookstore, or off my website at www.barbarawilson.org.

Whether you're going through this study on your own or in a group, it's important that you enlist a friend or mentor to be a support person for you on this journey. Ask God to bring to mind someone you can trust to love you and offer grace and compassion, not judgment. Someone who has a heart for God and will pray with and for you in the weeks ahead. Someone who can help you process what God is teaching you through this study, and will hold you accountable to all that God is asking you to do on this healing journey.

I encourage you to meet with this person once a week if possible, and be available by phone anytime. As much as we want to, we won't heal alone. Although God is the One who does the healing, He uses others to help. On my website, www.barbarawilson.org, there is a "support person guideline" sheet you can print off for your support person.

If you're married, you may want to let your husband know that you're taking this healing journey. Pick up a copy of my book, *Kiss Me Again: Restoring Lost Intimacy in Marriage*, from any bookstore or off my website, which will give you insight on how to share what you're learning with your husband and invite him to join you on this journey. On my website, www.barbarawilson.org, you'll find a special letter for husbands that you can print off to give to him.

I'm excited for you and incredibly proud of you. I'm excited that you're willing to allow God to restore what the enemy has stolen and destroyed in you. I'm proud that you're ready to stand with your head held high and live the victorious Christian life Jesus died for, that He rose from the dead for, that He lives in you for. I'm encouraged that you're anxious to embrace God's gift of grace and mercy, and allow it to replace the shame and pain you're living with. Even more, I'm humbled that God would use me to be a small part of what He wants to accomplish in your life.

So, take a deep breath, push back the fear and doubt, and jump in. And get ready for God to perform the greatest miracle of all, the miracle of His life-changing, healing work in you.

I'm praying for you,
Barb

CURRENT STATUS ASSESSMENT

Date: _____

Have you experienced any of the following (check all that apply):

_____ Schizophrenia	_____ Depression	_____ Mood Swings
_____ Anxiety/Panic Attacks	_____ Suicide or Attempts	_____ Sexual Abuse
_____ Physical Abuse	_____ Alcohol Abuse	_____ Imprisonment
_____ Learning Disability	_____ Attention Deficit	_____ Drug Abuse
_____ Dementia/Brain Damage	_____ Adoption	_____ Abortion
_____ Viewing Pornography	_____Baby born out of wedlock	
_____ Extra-Marital Affairs	_____ Cutting or Self Destructive Behaviors	

SYMPTOM & PROBLEM LIST
PLEASE CHECK THOSE THAT YOU ARE EXPERIENCING NOW

_____ No Energy	_____ Mood Swings	_____ Distractible
_____ Cannot Enjoy Life	_____ Unusual Experiences	_____ Sexual Indiscretions
_____ Memory Problems	_____ Physical Numbness	_____ Socially Withdrawn
_____ Anxiety	_____ Panic Attacks	_____ Eating Disorder
_____ Fatigue	_____ Vomiting	_____ Alcohol Use
_____ Anger Outbursts	_____ Drug Use	_____ Unsure of Reality
_____ Shortness of Breath	_____ Insomnia	_____ Wishing to Die
_____ Reliving Past Events	_____ Disturbing Memories	_____ Confusing
_____ No Loving Feelings	_____ Low Self-Esteem	_____ Weight Change
_____ Fears	_____ Poor Appetite	_____ Depressed
_____ Decisions Difficult	_____ Headache	_____ Guilt Feelings
_____ Racing Thoughts	_____ Flashbacks	_____ Poor Concentration
_____ Hard to Make Friends	_____ Nightmares	_____ Overeating
_____ Work Problems	_____ Hopeless Feelings	_____ Dizziness
_____ Out of Control Behavior	_____ Sexual Difficulties	_____ Unwanted Thoughts
_____ Suicidal Thoughts	_____ Hallucinations	_____ Sporadic Dieting
_____ Blackouts/Fainting	_____ Racing Heart	_____ Stomach Problems
_____ Sleeping Too Much	_____ Apathetic	_____ Numbing Out
_____ Distrustful	_____ Buying Sprees	_____ High Risk Activities
_____ Family Arguments	_____ Often Physically Sick	_____ Hearing Voices
_____ Losing Track of Time	_____ Slowed Thinking	_____ Physical Violence
_____ Unsure of Identity	_____ Taking Pain Killers Often	

Please list the three symptoms that trouble you most:

1. _____ 2. _____ 3. _____

SYMPTOM CHECKLIST[1]

Using the following guide, please evaluate those emotional, behavioral and physical responses you have experienced that may be related to past or present sexual damage. 0 = Not currently experiencing 1 = Mild 2 = Moderate 3 = Extreme		
DATE:	**Past**	**Now**
Have Difficulty Expressing Yourself Sexually		
Avoid times of intimacy		
Anxiety/Panic/Nervous Tension		
Feeling Numb (esp. during sex)		
Grief/Loss/Sorrow/Sadness		
Regret/Guilt/Shame		
Loneliness/Isolation/Difficulty Making friends		
Feeling "Branded" - As If Other People Can Tell		
Alienation/Feeling Different from Other People		
Depression/Hopelessness		
Have a General Mistrust of Men or Women		
Inability to Trust Myself or My Decisions/Self Doubt		
Anger/Rage		
Feelings of Having Been Victimized		
Feel Powerless to Assert /Protect Yourself against Sexual Harm		
Fear of Punishment		
Dreams/Nightmares/Difficulty Sleeping		
Fear or Discomfort with Sex or with Sexuality		
Seasons' or Cycles of Depression/Sickness/or Accident Prone		
Flashbacks or Hallucinations related to past experiences		
Difficulty Concentrating		
Secrecy/Difficulty Telling Others about Past		
Difficulty Forgetting and /or Difficulty remembering past sexual incidents		
Feeling 'Crazy'		
Crying Too Much or Too Easily/Inability to Cry		
Difficulty Bonding with or Overprotective of Children		
Do you struggle with eating too much or too little		
Increased Drug or Alcohol Use/Addiction		
Need to use Alcohol/Drugs to engage/enjoy sex		
Suicidal Thoughts/Attempts		
Fatigue/Tiredness		
Marital Difficulties/Marital Stress		
Need to be in Control		
Promiscuity (Many Sexual Partners)		
Feel Unworthy of Being Loved/Cared for		
Struggle with feelings of lust		
Tempted with Sexual Perversions		
Have Self Punishing Behaviors		
Struggle with Desiring /Enjoying Sex with Your Spouse		
Need to fantasize or use pornography to be sexually aroused		
Lowered Self-worth/Inferiority		
Struggle with Self/Other Contempt/Condemnation		

Your Current View of Sex

I want you to examine your current view of sex. In the space below, write about the feelings that you associate with sex, how you would describe your current view of sex. Write about what sex is, and isn't, for you--not about what you wish it was or what others say it is. Do not write about what you've read or heard sex should be, but how you feel about it right now. Don't spend too much time thinking about your answers. Simply write the first words that come to mind. Use present tense, as in sex is...

_____

_____

_____

_____

_____

_____

_____

_____

_____

_____

_____

_____

_____

_____

_____

_____

My Personal Goals For This Study

Date: _____

I'm trusting God to accomplish the following goals in me during this Bible Study:

1.

2.

3.

4.

5.

I'm willing to do the following things to make the above goals a reality:

1.

2.

3.

4.

5.

CHAPTER ONE

Knowing God

Day One: My View of God

What's your view of God? You have one--it may be obscure, but it's there. Throughout your life you've been absorbing data about God. Little by little, piece by piece, through life's experiences, people, and information you've been creating an image of who God is, what He's like and what He thinks of you. So stop and search your mind for a moment.

- If you were going to draw a picture of God, what would He look like?

- If you were going to write a bio for God, how would it read?

- If you were asked to list God's top ten character traits, what would they include?

- If you overheard God talking about you to Jesus, what would He say?

- Look back over your answers. Are you surprised? Did you discover something new about your view of God? Write your observations here:

Many of us have never stopped to examine our view of God. We've had it so long that we're oblivious to how we truly feel. I remember my first view of God. He certainly wasn't loving—unless of course I did something good. But that didn't happen often enough. In fact, I'd been rather bad growing up. I'm not talking about childhood stuff like lying, stealing and sticking out my tongue at my mother. (I got my mouth washed out with soap for that one.) I'm talking about what I assumed was the "unforgivable" stuff like premarital sex, divorce, abortion. You'll have to read my testimony in my book, *The Invisible Bond: How to break free from your sexual past* for the details.

I sensed that God liked to punish people—specifically me. So every day I'd try to be really good, and I'd ask Him to forgive me often—just in case today was *the* day. Worst of all, I was afraid He'd get angry with me. He had His rules and He had His reasons. I understood that--I just couldn't follow them too well.

It seemed that He only liked certain people. Like the ones who dressed properly for church—in their Sunday best. Because of all the church rules I had to follow, I assumed that His favorites didn't smoke, drink, play cards, go to dances or listen to the Devil's music— you know, Rock and Roll. And last but certainly not least, to keep from getting Him angry, you had to be in church absolutely *every* time anyone opened those doors for any reason. I didn't have a problem following those rules until I was ten. Things went downhill after that.

Does any of this ring true for you? Sadly, I wasn't ten when I discovered that I had the wrong view of God. I was thirty, married with three children. Even sadder, though I sensed it wasn't true I continued to let this skewed view of God keep me from getting close to Him.

- From your answers above, summarize your view of God.

- Read Psalm 103:6-17. How does the Psalmist describe God?

- How does your view of God differ or agree with His true character described in the above passage?

Regardless of our view of God, or who or what has influenced it, some of what we believe is true, and some is false. We may know the truth of God intellectually, but haven't experienced Him in our lives that way, which can skew our views of who He should be. Under the appropriate headings below, write what you believe is true about God from your present view, and what is not.

What is True	What is Not True

Where did it come from--this skewed view of God? Mine came from many places: my denomination, other Christians, my parents, preachers, my extended family, and Satan. Where did your view of God come from? Who or what has helped shape your image of God? This may be a hard one. Pray and ask God to reveal its source.

- Write your answer to the above questions here:

- What was your father like?

For many, our view of God comes from the character of our earthly father. If he was distant, abusive, hard or controlling, it may be why you view God in a similar fashion. Or if his love was conditional, based on your performance, it may be why you see God this way.

It's time to let Him vindicate His name and character. It's time to give up the lies and learn the truth. Believe me, it's time. I'm praying that as your present view of God is revealed, He will give you the faith to lay it down and embrace who He truly is.

Day Two: God's True Character

Who is God, really? What's He like? How can I get to know Him? Great questions. In the next few lessons we're going to answer these questions, and hopefully many others that you have about God.

However, first you need to know that God desperately wants *you* to know *Him*, intimately. That's why He pursues you and gives you a desire to know Him. You did not conjure up that desire yourself--that is one of God's incredible gifts. The yearning you have to know God is from Him. So let's begin our excursion--discovering the astonishing *true* character of God.

Names are important to God. Whenever He names someone in the Bible, it's designed to describe their character. The names of God do the same thing. Each one gives us a glimpse of who God is and what He's like. Let's look at just a few of the many names of God and see how He describes Himself. Read the following Scriptures and answer the questions.

Jehovah Tsidkenu—The Lord Our Righteousness

- Read 1 John 2:1-2 and 2 Corinthians 5:21. Jesus Christ is our Righteous One. What does He do for us?

- Read Romans 3:10-12. Why do we need Jesus to be righteousness for us?

- Read 1 John 1:9. What must we do to receive Jesus' gift of righteousness?

- Read Ezekiel 36:25-27. What is the result of the righteousness of Jesus?

- What in your past is not righteous?

- Were there some things done to you sexually that were not righteous?

The Bible says that Jesus, through His death on the cross, covers our sins with His righteousness. He covers everything we've ever done or will do. We need only accept His gift of righteousness by believing in what He's done for us, accepting His gift of salvation and asking Him to forgive us for all the sins we've ever committed. If you've never accepted Jesus' gift of forgiveness, than I invite you to pray the following prayer:

Dear Jesus:

I acknowledge that you are God. I believe that you died on the cross for my sins and that by accepting your gift of salvation, I am forgiven for all my past, present and future sins. I invite you into my life. I give you complete control of my life. Thank you for the gift of eternal life, which means that when I die I will live with you forever. Thank you for replacing my unrighteousness with your righteousness. It is an incredible gift. Thank you. Amen.

Welcome to the family of God! We're not perfect, but we're a big, loving body of believers. If you haven't already done so, you need to find a church family that teaches the truth of God's Word, actively promotes reaching the lost, provides opportunities for spiritual growth and equips people to serve Him.

Jehovah Shammah—The Lord is There

- What do the following verses say about God's presence?

Deuteronomy 31:6

Matthew 28:20

John 14:17

Hebrews 13:5

- How does it feel knowing that God is with you always?

- Do you believe God is with you even when you can't feel His presence? Why shouldn't we trust our feelings?

- What are some things we can do that will help us experience God's presence according to James 4:7-10?

- Do you believe God has always been with you—even during the events of your past? Why or why not?

One of the lies the enemy tries to deceive us with is that God is only around when things are going well. If we're experiencing trouble or pain then somehow God has left us. It's not true. When we allow our difficulties and worries to overwhelm us, we're tempted to exclude God. That can make us feel like God has left, but the one who left is us.

We leave God behind whenever we try to handle our struggles alone. Jesus promised that we'd have trouble in this world. In John 16:33 he says, *"I have told you these things, so that in me you may have peace. In this world you will have trouble. But take heart! I have overcome the world."* God doesn't promise to take away our trouble, but He does promise to walk through it with us.

- Read Isaiah 43:1-5. Why does God use the word 'when' in this passage? What does He promise to do when we're experiencing difficulties?

- Make a list of all the promises God has for you in the above passage.

The story is told of the sole survivor of a shipwreck that was washed up on a small, uninhabited island. He prayed feverishly for God to rescue him. Every day he scanned the horizon for help, but none seemed forthcoming. Exhausted, he eventually managed to build a little hut out of driftwood to protect him from the elements, and to store his few possessions.

One day, after scavenging for food, he arrived home to find his little hut in flames, with smoke rolling up to the sky. He felt the worst had happened, everything was lost. He was stunned with disbelief, grief, and anger. He cried out, "God! How could you do this to me?"

Early the next day, he was awakened by the sound of a ship approaching the island. It had come to rescue him. "How did you know I was here?" asked the weary man of his rescuers. "We saw your smoke signal," they replied.

The next time your hut is burning to the ground, don't lose heart. God is working behind the scenes, in the midst of your pain and suffering. Your burning hut may be the very smoke signal that summons God's victorious rescue.

Day Three: God's True Character--Part Two

Jehovah Rapha—The Lord Heals

- In your own words, describe God's promise to heal us from the following verses.

2 Chronicles 7:14

Psalm 103:1-5

Psalm 147:3

Isaiah 53:4-5

Isaiah 57:18-19

Isaiah 61:1-3

James 5:16

What do you need God to heal in you? Maybe you're not aware of the specifics of your need yet. That's okay and perfectly normal. God knows what we need more than we do. Pray and ask Him to reveal what needs healing in you. Maybe your need isn't apparent because you haven't put yourself in a position to hear from God.

- According to the verses above, what positions us to receive His healing?

Jehovah Jireh—The Lord Will Provide

- God provides us with everything that we need, emotionally, physically and spiritually. According to the following verses what does God provide for us?

Matthew 6:25-34

Acts 14:17

Romans 8:1-4

2 Corinthians 9:8

Philippians 4:4-7

Philippians 4:13, 19

1 Timothy 6:17

Ask God to show you how He has provided for you emotionally, physically and spiritually throughout your life. Write down some of the things that come to mind and write a prayer below to thank Him.

Regardless of what you've done in your past, God is your Righteousness. Despite how you feel, God is always with you. There is no wound too deep for Him to heal, and no need too great for Him to fill. God is your Righteousness, Healer, Provider and Constant Companion. You can believe Him, claim Him, trust Him. Why? Because there is nothing on earth more certain than Him.

Day Four: God's Amazing Love

Grasping even a fraction of the vastness of God's love will be necessary for you to trust Him with your past. The Bible says that we can't grasp it on our own—it's beyond our greatest imagination. That's because there is no human example of love that can compare to God's. Think about the person in your life who's shown you the greatest love. What qualities made their love so unique? How does their love make you feel?

Now imagine a love even greater, more self-less, more unconditional, more giving. Your highest thought of God's love is a mere sliver compared to the fullness of it. You'll never comprehend it alone. That's why you need the Holy Spirit to help you. Pray right now as you bask in God's love from these verses that the Holy Spirit will allow your mind to see the unimaginable, indescribable love of God—all for you.

Read the following verses and answer the questions:

- Psalm 103:11: What does the author mean when he says that God's love is higher than the heavens above the earth?

- Psalm 136: What does this Psalm say about God's love? How is it different from human love?

- Romans 5:5-8: How did God demonstrate His love for us? Why is that so significant?

- Romans 8:35-39: Have you felt separated from God's love because of your past? What does God say can separate us from His love?

- Ephesians 3:16-21: How is God's love described here? Who helps us "to know this love that surpasses knowledge?"

- 1 John 3:1: When was the last time you were "lavished" with love? God lavishes His love on us every day, but often we can't see it or receive it. Ask God to open your eyes and heart to "see" and "receive" His lavished love for you. Write down what He reveals to you.

- 1 John 4:7-10. What is unique about God's love from these verses?

- 1 John 4:8 says that God is love. 1 Corinthians 13:4-7 describes the characteristics of love and therefore describes the nature of God. I want you to rewrite 1 Corinthians 13:4-7 and replace the word love with the word God. You may also use "My Heavenly Father" in place of God.

Are you love-struck yet? Have you begun to grasp how much God loves you? Can you comprehend that God's love endures FOREVER, is greater than any love ever known? He offered it to you before you had the slightest thought of Him. Even after you rejected Him and went your own way, He still loved you. He's always loved you. He loved you then, He loves you now, and He'll continue to love you for all eternity.

It's amazing! You and I have done absolutely nothing to earn or deserve God's love. He loves us because of who *He* is. We can *try* to love others, but God *is* love. It's impossible for Him to be any other way.

Day Five: God's Unfailing Promises

I've been a Christian for forty-one years and I'm still discovering new and precious promises of God. I'm embarrassed to admit that they still surprise me. When God shows me something new about Himself, you think I'd remember that He's so much bigger than I can imagine. Yet each time, I wonder in awe that there could be *more*—more of His priceless promises and more of the gifts that He lavishly pours out on us.

There are so many promises, it will be impossible to mention them all in this lesson. I trust that the few we discover will compel you to search for the many more He has waiting to show you.

• In your own words write out the promise God has for you in each of the following verses. Read them again and see if there's something we need to do to receive His promise.

Psalm 91:2; 2

Psalm 103:1-5

Isaiah 40:28-31

Jeremiah 33:3

Matthew 7:7

John 3:16

John 14:15-18, 26

John 14:27

Romans 15:13

Ephesians 1:18-23

2 Thessalonians 2:16-17

2 Timothy 1:12

1 John 1:9

Forgive me for attempting to cram the character of our Holy, Almighty God into five lessons. I trust that my meager attempt will captivate your heart with renewed vision and love for Him. I can't even get my mind around the little bit I've shared with you, and God is so much, *much* bigger. I pray that it whets your appetite to seek Him with all your heart. When you do, He promises to show Himself to you. *Yes,* another promise! Jeremiah 29:13 says, "*You will seek me and find me when you seek me with all your heart. I will be found by you, declares the LORD.*" Get ready. Once you grasp the names, character and promises of God you'll never be the same.

Think About It...

- What's the most significant truth you've learned this week? Write out the verse (if applicable) that God used to speak to you.

- What is God asking you to do with this new truth?

- Write out your response (prayer) to God here:

CHAPTER TWO

Intimacy with God

Day One: Make a Date with God

What is the secret to making time with God our number one priority? If I could give you one simple step to transform your time with God from a sporadic duty to the best part of your day, would you be interested? Before you get concerned, I am not talking about a method or ritual that's a requirement in order for your quiet time to be successful. I'm suggesting a strategy that can make it easier for you to initiate and stay focused on your time with God. Our enemy, Satan, would like nothing more than to keep us from having consistent time with God. He knows how formidable and victorious we would be every day filled up with the knowledge and power of God's love. So we need a strategy, a plan to beat this enemy, and I have one for you.

My secret to making time with God a priority involves two important steps.

A Consistent Place or Sanctuary:

First, create a special place to meet with God. It needs to be in a quiet, undistracted area of your home. It could be a cozy chair, a window seat, even a walk-in-closet. Use the same place each time, and ideally (although not necessary) try not to use this place for anything else—like watching TV or eating, etc. Very soon you will begin to associate this special place with God—and it may very well become the favorite location in your house.

A consistent place will impact your quiet times in several ways. By having a special place, you're making a commitment to God to meet with Him—this will translate into greater consistency therefore increased spiritual benefit. Second, I find it helps me focus quicker and stay focused longer—which means less mind-wandering wasted time. Third, it gives you a place to keep your materials—Bible, notebook, pens, highlighters, journals, study guides, etc. Having everything there reduces the distraction of having to go around your house looking for things.

A consistent place has been the number one thing that has helped me and many others experience success in a daily quiet time. Don't by-pass this step. If you're not sure where your sanctuary is, ask God to show you as you tour your home in prayer.

Meet God Everyday

Make an appointment with God every day. If you can, try to meet in your special place at the same time every day. Individual schedules and internal time-clocks will need to be considered here. For some, mornings are best--for others, its evenings. I've tried several different times, and for me first thing in the morning works best. First, my mind is empty so I'm giving God the best time to speak to me—before the demands and plans of the day crowd in. Second, before anything happens in the day—before any worries, decisions, or relational challenges begin, I've surrendered myself and my day to God.

Now regardless of what comes my way, I'll see things through God's eyes, not mine. My circumstances may not change, but my perspective and my reactions will. Before I make any decisions, or talk to anyone, I want to be filled with the love, grace and peace of God through which all my words, thoughts and actions flow. Third, by going to God first, I'll have greater success at trusting Him throughout the day. Quite simply, that means less regret at the end of the day for things said, thought and done in my own strength.

Just two simple steps to get you started: a consistent place and meeting God every day. I've prepared a work sheet to help you. Use it as a guide and include God in your decisions-- after all, He is more eager to meet with you than you are with Him. He will want you to succeed, so I know He has an opinion on what your place and time should be.

Step 1: Find a location for your Sanctuary.

- Possible location(s) that could work:

- Obstacles I may face regarding this location(s):

- Supplies I have:

- Supplies I need:

Step 2: Decide on a time.

- Time of day that would work best for me:

- Obstacles I may face regarding this time:

- What sacrifice will I need make to keep this commitment (i.e. getting to bed earlier so I can get up earlier etc)?

Day Two: Learning to Read God's Word and Pray

Hopefully your special place is secured along with a specific time to meet with God. You've made the first step to increase your success in knowing God. Your effort in finding a place and time speaks volumes to God regarding your commitment to Him. Can you feel His pleasure? He is excited for you to know Him—He already knows everything about you.

Okay, you're in your special place--now what do you do? That's what this lesson will help you with. How do you get to know God? There isn't a right or wrong way. God made us unique individuals with different personalities, therefore how we relate to Him will be specific to us. But in saying that, there are some things that will help you learn to hear from God.

Step One: Surrender

> *"He wakens me morning by morning, wakens my ear to listen like one being taught."* (Isaiah 50:4b).

- In order to listen like one being taught, you need to come to your sanctuary time with a surrendered attitude.

- Surrender your quiet time to the Lord. Allow Him to lead what you will study and mediate on that day. To help you surrender, you may want to pray Psalm 25:4-5, "Show me **your** ways O Lord, teach me **your** paths, guide me in **your** truth and teach me, for you are God my Savior and my hope is in you all day long." The key is to surrender your plans, paths and what you think is truth to God, and ask Him to replace it with His plans, paths and truth.

- Surrender your heart, will, emotions, passions, desires, circumstances and day to the Lord. God has so much He wants to give us and teach us, but if we don't come surrendered and willing to be taught, we will leave empty.

- Ask God to search your heart for sin. Ask Him to show you where you have pride, and then ask Him to break you of that pride. A prayer I pray each day is, "Lord, break me where I have pride, and heal me where I'm broken."

Step Two: Silence

"The Sovereign Lord has opened my ears..." (Isaiah 50:5)

- *Listen*--Pick a passage from the Bible (example: Psalm 62:1-2). As you read, pray and ask God to speak to you through this passage. Then be still and listen with your heart and mind as God speaks to you. Carry on a two-way conversation with God, responding appropriately to what He is revealing to you (i.e. with thanksgiving or confession, etc.).

- *Journal*--Write down what God shares with you in your journal. When we write something down it becomes a part of us and we won't forget it. Plus, when God leads us to share what we've learned, we'll have it at our fingertips. I usually put the date and then write out the verse that stood out for me. I highlight the verse with a colored marker. After the verse, I write down whatever God revealed to me from this verse. Often I even write out a prayer in response.

Step Three: Respond

- *"... I have not been rebellious, I have not drawn back"* (Isaiah 50:5). When God speaks to us, He wants us to respond to Him by acting on what He's revealed. *Responding to God's Word involves not only hearing, but doing what the Bible says.* Pray and ask God to make what you learned today a part of your life, so that you will grow to be more like Him. When we ask God to use this in our life, then, like Isaiah, we are not being rebellious and not drawing back, but going forward to being more like Christ.

During this study, I want you to use your bible study week during your devotion time. This will give God ample opportunity to penetrate your heart and soul with His truth in the area of your sexuality throughout the day. At the end of each chapter there is an opportunity to write out what God has spoken to you that day--similar to the journaling mentioned above. This will get you in the habit of journaling what God is saying to you. You may also want to use a separate book to journal your answers.

Journaling is a crucial step—one not to by-pass. For all of us, regardless of whether we're visual or auditory learners, writing things down makes the lesson real and it guarantees that the Word of God is penetrating into the depths of our souls.

Day Three: Living in His Presence

The more time you spend with God and learn to hear from Him, the more you'll learn about Him, and the closer you'll feel to Him. I pray that as you practice this at least five times a week in accordance with your lessons, your meeting place becomes increasingly special to you, and your commitment to the same time becomes a daily habit. I've heard that in order to make a habit permanent you need to do it 21 days in a row. So don't give up if you're struggling. Each time you overcome whatever obstacle is determined to keep you from your commitment, God will give you more strength for the next time.

As you experience God's presence you may be tempted to believe that when you leave your sanctuary, you leave God behind. Not true. God is *in* us--all the time. Every moment of every day, wherever we go, God goes with us. When you leave your sanctuary and go into the kitchen to clean up, God is with you. When you get ready for work—He's there. At 3:30 p.m., when the activities of the day have crowded thoughts of Him to a distant memory— guess what, He's still there.

So, how do we practice living in His presence all day? Honestly, I'm still learning this. It's my greatest desire to live every moment in the awareness of His presence, but I think it's something that God is growing in me over time. I may continue to learn this until He takes me home to be with Him, but that's okay because I'm enjoying every step of this learning process.

- What do you learn about Christ's presence from these passages?

Psalm 139:1-12

Galatians 2:20

Ephesians 3:16-17

Colossians 1:27

Once we are convinced that Christ lives in us and is with us always, how can we live in that reality? I experience His presence in my sanctuary, but what about later in the day when everything is crazy or chaotic?

- Read Psalm 25:4-5. Where does David place his hope? When does he have this hope?

David hopes in God all day long. Regardless of how he's feeling, or what happens throughout his day, David has only one source of hope--God. He has a continual attitude of dependence on God. But how does he do that?

- Write out Proverbs 3:5-6.

- This is an amazing passage. I want you to memorize it. What three things does it tell us to do?

- When we lean on God and acknowledge Him, what will He do?

- Describe how you can trust the Lord with all your heart today in a practical way.

- What does it mean to "lean not on your own understanding?"

- Explain the phrase, "…in all your ways acknowledge Him."

- In what ways do you acknowledge God during the day?

- In what areas of your life do you need to start acknowledging God?

Webster defines trust as: "assured reliance on the character, ability, strength or truth of someone (or something)." When you trust in God with all your heart, you are depending on His character, His ability, His promises and His truth with all of your being—regardless of what is happening to you or around you.

I always remind myself that what I see happening is not always the truth. What God is doing behind the scenes is what is true. I may need to wait for it to come into my reality to see it, but I know its happening.

Day Four: Obedient Living

Obey—it's a scary word, isn't it? In a world where independence and strength are exalted, we struggle with having to surrender to someone else's control over us. Even to God. It's taken me awhile, but I've learned that I only experience God when I obey Him. You see, obedience takes faith—and God says our faith pleases Him. When I obey God, I demonstrate faith, which pleases God and He shows me more of Himself—which increases my faith so I can obey Him more.

- Read John 4:31-34, 12:49, 50 and 14:31. Who modeled obedience for us?

- Why did He obey His Father?

- Why did Jesus compare obedience to food?

- How can we show our love to God according to John 14:15-21?

- Read Luke 6:46-49. What does God call someone who hears His words and puts them into practice?

- How is the wise man different from the foolish man?

What's the difference between the foundations of the wise man and the foolish man? Look closely. It's not that the foolish man has a poor foundation compared to the wise man's solid foundation—instead the foolish man has *no* foundation at all. When we only *hear* God's words without putting them into practice, we go from a solid foundation to no foundation at all.

In Michael Wells' book, *Problems, God's Presence and Prayer,* he says that obedience is the difference between feeling empty or full. According to Wells, when we become a child of God, and Christ comes to dwell in us, we now long for obedience—it's what completely satisfies us. Obedience doesn't make us more acceptable to God, but it determines whether we live satisfied or unsatisfied.

Wells goes on to say, "When it comes to the preference of disobedience versus obedience, it is merely a choice between eating dog food, or steak and lobster. Dog food will not satisfy; steak and lobster will!...Do you want to be full? Then obey! For obedience is what you are craving…Once we see obedience as the true food for which we long, in every situation we will begin to ask ourselves, 'Do I want to be full or not? Do I want to be satisfied?'…The Jesus who stated what His true food was, is the very same Jesus with the very same appetite that lives within you. You know what to feed His life, so you can always find the joy of being satisfied."[2]

You've already taken a step of obedience by trusting God with your past. God will be asking you to obey Him in other ways throughout this study. How are you going to respond? Keep in mind that until we obey, we will feel empty and unsatisfied in the depth of our souls. Christ in us longs for obedience—it is the doorway to living the abundant Christian life.

- What is God asking you to do that you haven't obeyed yet?

What is keeping you from obeying God? Surrender your fear of obedience to God and ask Him to give you the desire, courage and strength to obey.

Day Five: Abundant Living

What a week! How are you doing so far? Do you have a sanctuary? Have you discovered a consistent time that works best? If so, then I'm excited for you. You have begun a path that's addicting—in a good way. With each step you take on this journey, the farther you'll want to go.

The more you get to know God, the more of Him you'll want to know. Every time you obey Him, you experience Him in a new way, and the more eager you'll be to obey again—and *again*. This path you're on has a name—it's called the Abundant Life. In other words, living a life of heaven here on earth. It's one of God's incredible gifts.

- Read John 10:10. Who is the thief? What has he come to do?

- What in your life has the thief killed? Stolen? Destroyed?

- What people or circumstances did the thief use in your life to steal, kill and destroy?

- What do you think made you vulnerable to the thief's tactics?

- Who said, "I have come that they may have life and have it abundantly (to the full)"?

- How is this statement different from what the thief has in mind?

- Look up abundant in the dictionary. Write out the definition here.

- Take a moment and dream. What's your idea of an abundant life?

Have you written down your dream life? Did you know that God wants to exceed your wildest dreams? Yes! Dream as big as you can—and then know that God wants to exceed even that. Maybe not in the way you think or know, but in ways that you've never thought of. I'm not making it up—God said it.

- Read Ephesians 3:20. Write it out here:

God is *able* to do immeasurably more than all we could ever ask or imagine—does that blow your mind? It should, because your biggest thought or wildest dream is only the beginning to Him.

- Fill in the blanks: "Now to Him who is able to do immeasurably more than all we ask or imagine according to _____ that is at work _____."

- How does God exceed our wildest imaginations?

- Where is that power residing?

Not only does God want to do wild, unimaginable things in your life, relationships, marriage and future, He also wants to accomplish wild, unimaginable changes inside *you*.

- What unimaginable changes would you like God to work inside you?

The abundant life isn't about having a big house, fancy cars, perfect children, perfect marriage, or perfect career—you get the picture. The abundant life is to live with a love, joy, peace and hope that transcends human understanding especially when everything else isn't perfect.

That's the miracle and mystery of the abundant life in Christ. I can have peace whether the bank account is full or empty. There's deep joy that lasts long after the temporary happiness of a new toy is gone. I have hope even when the situation seems hopeless, and there's unconditional love for the most unlovable person in my life. When I am living in an abundance of peace, joy, love and hope regardless of my circumstances, I am *truly* living. It's a life that surpasses everything I know. It transcends my humble understanding. It exceeds my wildest imagination. It satisfies my deepest longings, and it's available inside you and inside me—*right now*. What's keeping you from taking hold of the abundant life God is offering? As you close today, pray and ask Him to show you.

Think About It...

- What's the most significant truth you've learned this week? Write out the verse (if applicable) that God used to speak to you.

- What is God asking you to do with this new truth?

- Write out your response (prayer) to God here:

CHAPTER THREE

Acknowledging Your Past

Day One: Examining My Past

Sex is like glue—super human glue. God never intended for humans to have multiple sexual partners. Instead he designed and created our bodies, souls, minds and spirits to be sexually bonded for life with one partner in marriage.

"But what's the big deal?" you may be asking, "It's only sex. How does breaking one relationship and moving on to another have anything to do with my mind, body, soul or spirit?" Or perhaps you're married now and the past sexual relationships are just that—past, done, out of sight, out of mind. You've asked God to forgive you for those—how can they impact you now?

God says in his Word that when we engage in the intimate act of sexual relations with someone, we become *one* with them, a complete, all-encompassing union in our minds, souls and spirits as well as our bodies. So what happens when we become *one* with multiple partners?

Physically, our body, affection and attention may move on to someone new after a breakup, but what about our souls, spirits and minds? Are they able to put the past behind so easily? Can every part of me move into the next relationship, brand new without residue attached from the previous ones? If there is sexual residue, what does it consist of? How does it impact me now or in future relationships?

Great questions. I have an exercise to see if you can discover the answers yourself. First, take a moment and think back to your very first sexual experience. You may need to ask God to help you remember some of the details especially, if you've buried it deep because of pain or shame.[3]

- Were you married or single? An adult, teen or child?

- Were you in a serious relationship, or was it a one-night stand?

- Was it consensual, or were you a victim?

- If your first experience was as a child in the case of sexual abuse, did you become sexually promiscuous as a teen, young adult, or during or after marriage?

- Would you characterize your first relationship as positive or negative?

- How painful was the break-up for you?

- After you broke up, how soon did you initiate sex in your next relationship?

- If you waited for marriage to have sex, but then later divorced, did you become promiscuous prior to your second marriage?

- What about a second relationship, third, fourth and so on? How many sexual partners have you had?

- You may be in a committed, loving marriage relationship right now, but sometimes when you make love do the faces of past lovers flash through your mind? And then do you find yourself comparing your spouse's love making abilities with those better or worse from the past?

- Do you often find yourself fantasizing about past lovers—what if I had married him or her instead of the one I did?

- Are you in a second or third marriage only to find history repeating itself? "What is wrong with me," you ask? "Why can't I pick the right one?"

- Did you find yourself enjoying sex before you were married, but now it's not so exciting? Or do you have to conjure up pornographic images to get aroused during love-making?

- Do you find that even though you're married you can't resist flirting with the opposite sex and desiring their attention?

- Do you experience shame and regret when you think about your past sexual relationships? And are you afraid that someone will find out?

- Do you struggle with trust, faithfulness, commitment and emotional intimacy in relationships?

Did you see yourself in that long but not all-inclusive list? Can you relate to any of these scenarios? At this point you may be wondering: what's the big deal with sexual bonding? It has the potential to alter your view of yourself, others and sex. It can propel you on a destructive course of promiscuity and other high-risk behaviors. It can impair your ability to choose healthy people to date and marry. It can lead to sexual addiction or dysfunction. And it can affect your ability to have close and intimate relationships with others and with God. It also leaves the most painful wounds.

Inside marriage, God designed sex to be a bond that is powerful and unifying. Outside marriage, the bonds of sex can be devastating. Long after the lover has gone, the bond we've created stays with us, impacting our lives and future relationships in a negative way.

Research shows that teenagers who began sexual activity at a young age and have multiple partners are less than half as likely to have stable committed relationships in their thirties than someone who waited to initiate sex later in life.[4] The greater number of sexual partners, the greater the residue, and the greater the impact.

- From the questions above, what has God revealed to you about some of the sexual residue that has impacted you?

- Do you believe that God can free you from your past and renew, restore and rebuild your life and relationships?

- What is the one thing God is asking you to trust Him with today?

Day Two: Exposing the Wounds

Our sexual pasts don't just impact our choices in the present and future, but also our emotions, our thoughts and our attitudes. The wounding goes deep. It can cause us to close up spiritually, emotionally and physically to protect ourselves from further wounding. This happens in various ways. It comes out of a need to guard our hearts from further pain.

I have some more questions for you. Pray and ask God to help you truly see where your wounds are. I pray He'll give you the courage to be honest with yourself and Him. Don't be afraid—He knows it all anyways, and loves you just the same.

For this exercise, I want you to go back and review two of the assessment sheets you did at the beginning of this study: the current status and symptom checklist. If you haven't already filled these out, do it now. As you look through what you've checked, answer these questions:

1. Looking at the top part of the Current Status sheet, what are the events that have happened in your life up to this point? Write out all that apply in the past or currently.

2. Looking at the items you checked in the second part of the Current Status sheet, list the top five that are causing you the most concern right now.

   1)

   2)

   3)

   4)

   5)

3. Looking at the Symptom Checklist, list the items that you marked with a 2 or 3.

As you look over these two sheets, this reflects you right now. Sometimes we can survive for years, not realizing how the wounds from our past are impacting us today. But don't despair. Recognizing our current struggles is the beginning step to surrendering them to God and letting Him heal all of them. As you continue to examine your lists, consider these questions:

1. What sexual trauma did you experience as a child? As a teen? Young adult? Adult?

2. Which one was the most traumatic for you?

3. What sexually destructive behavior are you currently involved in?

4. How did your mother influence your understanding of sex? Women? Love? Marriage?

5. How did your father influence your understanding of sex? Men? Love? Marriage?

6. As you examine the events of your past, in which were you a victim?

7. Which events resulted from your own choices?

8. What are some of the lies about sex, yourself and others that have become ingrained in you because of your experiences?

9. How have those lies contributed to your attitude towards sex? Toward yourself? Toward others? (men, women, spouse)

10. How has your past impacted your relationship with God? Did it drive you to Him or away from Him?

When I answered these questions, God began to reveal some of the lies that I had embraced about sex, men and myself through my experiences. My very first sexual encounter was definitely traumatic. Even though it wasn't rape, it was done in a hurried and secretive manner in a not so public place. There was little care for my feelings, or comfort from this guy who was supposed to love me. I sensed his need to get the job done regardless of how I was feeling. It was a very humiliating, vulnerable experience and I didn't realize it until I answered the above questions. Whatever feelings I experienced that day must have been locked away because this was the first I was aware of them.

What did that have to do with me right now? Everything. God showed me that my view of sex had been shaped by that experience. Somewhere in the back of my conscience, sex was a humiliating and vulnerable experience and guys didn't really care about how you felt as long as they got what they wanted. Unconsciously, I had imposed that attribute onto my husband and brought that attitude into our bed.

I'm praying that as God reveals your past with all its pain, shame, residue and consequences, you will experience hope not only in His passionate desire to free you, but also in His Almighty power to deliver you.

Day Three: Making a Sexual History List[5]

One of the steps God led me through in my healing process was to write out my sexual history list and pray a prayer asking God to break the sexual bonds I'd created. I know that might sound unpleasant or scary, but believe me when I say that God has used this important step in everyone I've walked through sexual healing. There's nothing magic about the prayer. Instead it's the faith in which you utter the words. You must have faith that God will break the ties you have made so you can give yourself wholly and completely to Him.

To start, get alone with God and open to Psalm 139. Bask in the incredible truth that God knows you completely. He sees you right where you're sitting. The Bible says that He sees you when you get up, walk around or get in your car. Before a word is on your tongue or a thought is in your mind, He already knows it. He created you in the secret place of your mother's womb. He designed how you'd look, how you'd think and feel, and what your gifts would be. All the days of your life He ordained before one of them came to be.

David says that this is too wonderful for him to grasp—too amazing, too precious. As you ask God to reveal the names, faces and events of your sexual past, remember that He already knows everything about you. He knew it before any of it happened. And guess what—He doesn't love you any less now than before.

As you pray, God will bring to mind those you've forgotten, denied, or purposely removed from your memory because of pain and shame. Allow Him to remind you of all the bonds created in your past that you need healing from. It will certainly include everyone you've had sex with outside of marriage—homosexual lovers as well as heterosexual ones.

The list may also include those you've had emotional, fantasizing affairs with, and those whom you did everything but have intercourse with. Some of the faces God reveals may include fake people--those on the internet, in a magazine, on the phone or in a video. These are images you've become bonded to through pornographic sex. God may bring to mind the faces of those who used you for their pleasure against your will through rape or sexual abuse. Your list will include one-night stands as well as long, committed relationships--those you were too drunk to know and ones you knew very well. It will also include those you married and divorced and the ones you just lived with. It will even include the one you're married to right now if you had sex with them before you were married.

This is where most people get stuck.

"My list is longer than I imagined," they lament.

"I'll never get through it all."

"God will never forgive all this."

This is exactly where the enemy wants you to stay—on the other side of the door to healing. This will be the hardest part. Give God a chance. He knows what needs revealing, how much time you'll need, and how much courage is required to face what you must see.

Write down everything God shows you. If you don't know a name, write down where you were, what you did—anything you remember. This is an important part of the process. We can no longer be deceived that it never happened when we see it in black and white.

Don't be discouraged if it takes several tries to complete your list. Part of the healing process is grieving what you've done and what you've lost. You may feel sad or depressed. You may be reluctant to return to your list once you've begun. Don't despair. Grieving is God's way of allowing us to feel the pain so that He can comfort and restore us. Be assured as you grieve, the Holy Spirit within is grieving right along with you. We have a compassionate God, one who wants to lift our heavy burden and place it on Himself. In exchange He offers comfort, healing and love. Let Him have your pain. He is trustworthy. You can trust that He'll reveal everything you need to see when you need to see it. He knows the pace that's right for you.

I want you to take time over the next few weeks and allow God to continue to show you events, names and faces that need to be on your list. Eventually we will pray and ask God to break those bonds we've created, but for now I want you to focus your attention on making the list and writing it down.

A concern for many of you is the possibility of someone finding it. That can be very scary. I know. Keep your list or your study in a private place where unwanted eyes can't find it. If you want to type your story or list on a laptop or PC, you can protect your document with a password. To do this in Word, click on tools, then options, and then security. You can put in a password that will keep others from reading your document.

Summary: Breaking the Ties

- Ask God to bring to mind everyone that you've had sexual contact with—voluntarily or involuntarily. Wait quietly, allowing God to bring names to memory.

- Write down each name. If you don't know the name, write down a description of the person or event. Use the next page or a separate page if you'd like.

Day Four: Telling Your Story

"Therefore, since Christ suffered in his body, arm yourselves also with the same attitude, because he who has suffered in his body is done with sin. As a result, he does not live the rest of his earthly life for evil human desires, but rather for the will of God." (1 Peter 4:1-2).

What I asked you to do yesterday and what I'm asking you to do today is painful. I'm sorry about that. But the truth is, the pain you're experiencing because of these exercises is really good pain. The pain we live with day after day as a consequence of our past sexual choices and trauma is bad pain. It's the pain that keeps us stuck emotionally, spiritually and physically--just trying to survive. We hope that if this pain never goes away, then at least it won't get any worse. In contrast, as we heal, the good pain, though raw and gut-wrenching, completely eradicates the bad pain that continues to re-wound us.

Bad pain attacks us and puts us on the defense, while good pain is something we initiate. In other words, we go on the offense with the pain. We take it on, making the pain work *for* us rather than *against* us.

In one of the most enlightening books I've ever read, *How People Grow,* Drs. Henry Cloud and John Townsend spend a whole chapter on the absolute necessity of embracing pain in order to heal. They describe these two kinds of pain—good and bad. They explain that, "The bad pain comes from repeating old patterns that help us avoid the suffering it would take to change…bad pain is really wasted pain. It is the pain we go through to avoid the good pain of growth that comes from pushing through."[6] In other words the bad pain is really our way of self medicating instead of dealing with the pain.

In contrast, good pain leads to healing. When we expose our pain it hurts. But in the exposure, God is able to shine his light of truth on every aspect of it and then true healing occurs. This is difficult because our natural tendency is to avoid pain. But avoidance blocks the healing. In 1Peter 4:1-2, Jesus not only talks about suffering but models it.

Christ's attitude was to embrace suffering—not avoid it. He knew the redemptive quality of suffering, and was willing to endure it completely and thoroughly so that we would know its healing power. Watching the movie, *The Passion of the Christ,* was an intense, emotional experience from beginning to end, but there is one scene that continues to play over and over in my mind. It is when Christ is being beaten with His hands tied to the stake. The beatings cause His blood-soaked, semi-conscious body to collapse to the ground. He could have stayed on the ground and the beatings would have stopped. They never beat someone to death, just to the door of death. Staying down would have ended the beatings. What Jesus did next will forever be ingrained on my heart and mind.

He got up. He pulled himself to His feet and stood as tall as his broken, bleeding body would allow, knowing full well that they would have to continue beating Him. The guards were stunned, and so was I. With reluctance, the soldiers resumed the most brutal beating I imagine any human has endured. What made Him do that? I would have stayed on the ground—avoiding more beatings, and more pain. But He didn't. What an incredible model of suffering He is for us. Christ purposefully embraced all of the pain necessary so that our healing would be complete.[7]

- Write out 1 Peter 4:1-2 here:

- *"Therefore since Christ suffered in his body…"* Take a moment and thank Jesus for suffering in His body for you. Isaiah 53:5 says, "*…by His wounds we are healed."* Jesus suffered so you could be healed and set free. What do you want to say to Jesus for what He's done for you?

- *"…arm yourselves also with the same attitude…"* By having the same attitude as Christ and embracing the good pain of healing, God says we are arming ourselves against the endless destructive cycle of that sin or habit or stronghold. How can our pain be armor for us?

- "…because he who has suffered in his body is done with sin…" What sin/habit/struggle/stronghold would you like to be done with?

- How will suffering in your body help you be done with it?

If you're doing this study in a group, you'll have an opportunity to share your story with your group this week. If you're doing it on your own, I encourage you to share your story with your support person, a trusted friend, pastor or mentor. This is an important step in your healing journey. We'll talk more about the importance of this step in tomorrow's lesson.

It's very important that you write your story out. Just thinking about it in your mind is not as effective. Writing out the details of your story makes it real. Having it in front of you in black and white brings it to life. Seeing your story allows God to separate what's true from the lies you've believed. Then by sharing your story with others you are set free from the full weight of this burden you've had to carry your whole life, and you allow others to share in that burden. And most important, God allows you to experience unconditional love and grace through those in the body of believers you share with.

Please use the following guide and your answers from this week to help you write out your story. Don't be concerned about hitting every point. Just allow the following questions to help you get started and provide direction. Once you begin, the Holy Spirit will take over and the words will flow.

- What is your first memory of being exposed to sex? Describe the circumstances surrounding that memory: when, where, how, by whom, and how old you were.

- Tell us about your first sexual experience: with whom, where, when, and any significant circumstances surrounding it.

- How did that first experience impact the choices you made in your life?

- What are some of the consequences of your past sexual experiences that still affect you today?

- What are your feelings now regarding your past sexual experiences?

- Have you had any counseling or prior healing in this area?

Day Five: The Need for Forgiveness and Healing

What makes sexual sin different from stealing or lying? Why is it that we still feel the wounds of sexual sin decades later, but are able to let go of the shame of a lie with a simple confession. I Corinthians 6:18 says, *"Flee sexual immorality. All other sins a man commits are outside the body, but he who sins sexually sins against his own body."*

Although sexual sin is not worse than other sins, it is different. The Bible says it's the only sin that we commit against our own body. This means that even with forgiveness the wounding of sexual sin can continue to negatively impact us decades later unless healing accompanies it.

- Read 1 John 1:9. Explain why the first word of this verse is 'if'.

- What will Jesus do "if we confess our sins?"

- Read James 5:16. Jesus says that when we confess our sins to Him, He forgives us. According to this verse, what happens when we confess our sins to each other?

- Why does God make it necessary for us to experience healing through others?

- Read Mark 5:24-34. Why did the woman plan to secretly touch Jesus' garment rather then ask Him for healing?

- Why did Jesus ask who had touched Him when He already knew?

- Why did Jesus want the woman to come forward publicly?

- Why did the woman come trembling with fear before Jesus? What was she afraid of?

This poor woman had been subject to bleeding for twelve years. She suffered a great deal under the care of many doctors and spent all she had, yet instead of getting better she got worse. That's not all. In her culture, the bleeding condition made her unclean, therefore untouchable. Because of this she was condemned to a lonely life of shame and pain. Knowing about Jesus, she thought, "If I just touch his clothes, I will be healed."

The moment she touched Jesus' garment she was healed. But then the story gets interesting. She tried to retreat back into the crowd and go away unnoticed. But Jesus didn't allow her to. Immediately He turned and said, "Who touched me?" Of course, Jesus already knew who touched Him. So why insist that she come forward and expose herself to Him and all the people? Why was that so important? How would this help in her healing?

First of all, her healing had only been physical. Jesus also wanted to forgive her sins and heal her spiritually. This is what I love about God. He always wants to exceed our expectations, not just meet them. Her expectations were for physical healing, but Jesus exceeded that by providing her not only with healing here and now, but an eternal life free from suffering by forgiving her sins.

Secondly, the fact that He stopped and took the time to hear her whole story made it *real*. It really happened. Later, alone, the enemy would never be able to convince her that it never happened, that she'd only just imagined it. Forever etched in her memory would be the sound of His voice, the touch of His hand, and the gentle look of love in His eyes as He pronounced her healed and forgiven. The enemy had just been defeated, the bonds to her past broken, and no one would ever be able to convince her otherwise.

Not now.

Finally, she came to know Jesus in a whole new way. She knew He was a miracle worker, but she didn't know that He was compassionate, loving, and forgiving. The passage says she came and fell at His feet, trembling with fear. What was she afraid of--maybe humbling herself and coming forward, the hardest thing of all? I hear it from people all the time. "Oh I know I'm forgiven, but I can't tell anyone because I'm a private person."

I can relate to how this woman felt. I know what I was afraid of--that people would reject me, cast their judgmental stones at me, and deem me unworthy of their respect and love.

But I think she was also afraid of Jesus. Maybe He would be angry with her and take His power and healing back. Or even worse, maybe He'd punish her. Have you ever been afraid that if you really own up to what you've done, God would reward you with even greater consequences? I did. That thought kept me from drawing closer to God even when I knew He was calling me. Maybe if I can just forget it, put it out of my mind, it would all go away and I'd never have to deal with it.

But it didn't work for this woman, it didn't work for me, and it won't work for you. Every time we reach out to God, His great love and compassion compels Him to heal and forgive us completely. Just like this woman, that means coming humbly before Him, falling at His feet, and giving Him permission to do whatever it takes.

That's why God asks us to humble ourselves before Him and others by sharing our sins, shame and pain. It's through others in the body of Christ that God will hear us and heal us.

Maybe like me you've spent years asking God to forgive you, but because you weren't healed you couldn't receive that forgiveness. If so, then expect something incredible as you share your story this week. No, He probably won't speak audibly to you or suddenly appear and call you forward. But you will experience your burden lifted and exchanged with His immeasurable grace, pleasure and love through those in His body. All because you were willing to trust Him, instead of yourself.

You may, like the bleeding woman, be trembling with fear this week as you anticipate sharing your story. But like her you'll also discover that with Jesus making the request, your fear is always unfounded.

Think About It...

- What's the most significant truth you've learned this week? Write out the verse (if applicable) that God used to speak to you.

- What is God asking you to do with this new truth?

- Write out your response (prayer) to God here:

CHAPTER FOUR

Addressing the Present

Day One: God's Prohibitions

The secret to living free is living within boundaries—God's boundaries. Sounds like an oxymoron doesn't it? Our vision of freedom is a life without boundaries, without restrictions. But the opposite is true. God gives us boundaries not to stifle our freedom but to ensure it. His boundaries are designed to protect and provide us with the abundant, fulfilling life He wants for us. His boundaries keep us on the path to life—the path to freedom. King David in Psalms knew all about the freedom of boundaries.

- Read Psalm 16:5-6. How does David describe God's boundaries? What does he say they provide for him?

- According to verse 5, how do the boundaries make him feel?

When you went to elementary school did you have a fence around your playground? Most of us did. The fence not only kept us from wandering too far away from the school but also kept people intending to harm us from coming in. I heard a true story of a school that decided to take down their fence. They noticed that the children liked to play around the fence and interpreted this to mean that they would like a more unrestricted area to play in. The first day without a fence, the children ran out enthusiastically for recess but stopped short when they discovered the new playground. The administration assumed the children would love the freedom of the playground, but the opposite happened. Rather than feeling free to go to the edge of the playground, the children all huddled together in the center. The absence of the fence meant that now they were uncertain of what the boundary was, and so did not venture out beyond the middle of the playground.

The fence had given them a boundary of how far they could go, making them feel secure in their surroundings. Without it they had to decipher the boundaries on their own, leaving them unsure and wary.

That's what God's boundaries do for us. They make us secure in what is right and good and which way we're supposed to go. God's boundaries have other names. In Psalm 19 David describes God's boundaries with words like law, statutes, precepts, commands and ordinances.

- Read Psalm 19:7-11. How are God's boundaries described here? What's the result of trusting in God's laws, statutes, precepts, commands and ordinances?

So what are God's boundaries regarding sex? Linda Dillow and Lorraine Pintus in their book, *Intimate Issues*[8], give us God's ten "sex" prohibitions—His absolute "thou shalt not" list. Read through the list and look up the verses. Ask God to show you if there is anything that you are participating in on this list that you need to eliminate from your life.

1. Fornication—1 Corinthians 6:15-20. Fornication is any sex outside a monogamous marriage relationship.

2. Adultery—Leviticus 20:10, Matthew 5:27-28. Adultery can be mental and physical. Fantasizing about having sex with someone is the same as actually having sex with someone else's spouse according to God. Adultery is similar to fornication in that whenever you're having sex with someone who is not your spouse (even if you're not married), it's considered adultery.

3. Homosexuality—Leviticus 18:22, Romans 1:27.

4. Impurity— 1 Corinthians 6:9. Moral uncleanness in action, thought or deed.

5. Orgies—whether married or single, sexual orgies involving group sex is wrong according to items 1, 2, and 4 above.

6. Prostitution – Leviticus 19:29, Proverbs 7:4-27.

7. Lustful passions—Mark 7:21-22, Ephesians 4:19. Unrestrained, indiscriminate sexual desire for men or women other than the person's marriage partner.

8. Sodomy—the biblical meaning for sodomy is "men lying with men." The English term means "unnatural sexual intercourse especially of one man with another or of a human being with an animal."

9. Obscenity and coarse jokes—Ephesians 4:29, Ephesians 5:4.

10. Incest—Leviticus 18:7-18; 20:11-21.

There is no question that the above items are wrong according to God. But unfortunately in our culture there is much ambiguity regarding sex. I'm sure you have many questions that haven't been answered by this list. Questions like, is masturbation wrong? What about pornography in marriage, before marriage? In the days ahead we'll tackle these issues and provide tools to help you discern God's will in these issues and others you may be experiencing.

In the meantime, thank God for His boundaries that keep you protected and secure and on the path to living free.

Day Two: Caution Areas

Have you noticed that sex is rarely just about sex? The world would like us to think so-- that would make it less complicated and innocent, wouldn't it? But the truth is our desire for sex or lack thereof rarely has anything to do with the act of sex. Like glue, sex adheres to our minds, souls, emotions, and spirits dictating how we view God, others, ourselves and sex.

And so we struggle in our silent prisons wondering what's okay and what's not. What's wrong with me? Why don't I like sex? Why do I like it so much? Am I a pervert? Am I the only one that struggles with this? Can I ever be free from these thoughts, desires, and actions?

Enough of the silent struggles. It's time to bring all your questions, struggles and secrets into God's light so that you can know the truth--especially the truth about sexual things God does not directly address in His Word. But how can we discern God's will when He doesn't give us clear boundaries on the topic? It seems like the world is always inventing new ways to ensure that our struggle with sex gets more complicated, more secret, more perverse.

I've got good news. God does give tools to help us discern His will regarding even the most complicated sexual struggle. Everything you're wrestling with, God has an answer for. So let's begin. Some may be obvious—while others will take more study, prayer and meditation before your answer is clear.

When you have an issue that the Bible doesn't clearly address, there are three questions Dillow and Pintus suggest you should ask yourself.

1. Is it prohibited in Scripture? If not we may assume it is permitted.

• Read 1 Corinthians 6:12. Write out the verse here:

If what you're struggling with comes under one of the ten on God's prohibited list then there's no need to search any further. You have your answer. We often like to rationalize our situation before God and say, "Yes God, but our situation is a little different."

It won't work. I remember counseling with a young, pregnant Christian girl who had her fiancé move in with her before their marriage. She said that while praying about it, God had told her this was His will. I'm sorry, but that wasn't God's voice she was listening to. God would never tell us to do something that is contrary to His Word. If you've asked God and searched the Scripture and you find a clear "thou shalt not" on the issue—the case is closed. Don't try to bargain with God or convince Him of your "extenuating" circumstances. His no is no.

2. *Is it beneficial?*

First Corinthians 6:12 goes on to say, "Everything is permissible for me—but not everything is beneficial." If something is beneficial it will contribute to our spiritual, social, emotional and physical well being. How do we know if something is beneficial? That's a little harder, but here is where God is faithful to show us even when we're not asking. If you're a Christian, you have the Spirit of God living in you. Whenever you're doing something that is not beneficial to you, He will let you know. And even if you're not listening—the results of your actions will show you. If God can't get your attention through His Word or prayer, then He'll use your consequences to make you miserable, feel convicted, and make others in your life feel miserable as well. Hopefully in the next couple of days you'll gain some tools to help you become discerning in this area. In the area of sex—if the action harms the husband or wife, or the sexual or marriage relationship in any way, then it should be rejected.

3. *Does it involve anyone else?*

Sexual activity is sanctioned by God for husband and wife only. If a sexual practice involves someone else or becomes public, it is wrong. This is based on Hebrews 13:4 which warns us to keep the marriage bed undefiled. "Marriage should be honored by all and the marriage bed kept pure…" (Hebrews 13:4).

Now that we have the tools, we're going to look at some of the not so obvious sexual struggles we face today. For now, ask God what you're struggling with sexually that would benefit from the scrutiny of these three questions. You probably already know the answer—but then again you may be surprised.

Day Three: Pornography

Some of you may be surprised that I've included pornography as a caution area rather than under God's prohibitions. "It's obviously wrong," I can hear you say. But for others it may not be so clear—even as Christians. I attended a marriage conference where the speaker (who happened to be our pastor) said that whatever you did sexually in marriage was okay as long as you both were comfortable with it. Christian friends of ours encouraged the use of pornography in marriage, saying that it enhanced their sexual relationship—and because they were married and were watching it together, it was acceptable. I even had a woman come up to me after a seminar I gave and say that her doctor had encouraged her and her husband to view pornography during their love-making to spice up their sex life.

So is pornography unacceptable when you're viewing it alone, but acceptable when you're watching it together in marriage? What do you think? Why don't we examine it using our three questions?

- *Is it prohibited in Scripture?* Go back and read God's prohibitions from Day One. Which of the ten items could apply to pornography? List them here:

I believe that viewing pornography is prohibited by God based on numbers 4, 7 and 9 of God's ten prohibitions for sex. Viewing pornography starts in our thoughts—but as we continue to dwell on it, the images permeate our attitudes, words and actions as well. Pornography is Satan's way of taking what God meant as good, sacred and pure and making it perverse and public. Not only is pornography considered obscene material—even by worldly standards, it also stimulates impure thoughts and actions, and leads to lustful passions toward people other than your spouse or future spouse.

- *Is it beneficial?* If you haven't already done so, read Chapter Three in *The Invisible Bond*. As you read, consider what some of the dangers of watching pornography are before marriage, in marriage and as a child.

Before marriage, as you've read in *The Invisible Bond*, viewing pornography creates a bond to an actual picture, fantasy or image in our minds. Over time this bond trains the brain to have an arousal response to these pictures or images rather than a live person. This is why many who become addicted to pornography continue the practice into their marriages. Many couples are devastated and marriages destroyed because of pornography that started long before the couple ever met. Remaining a virgin for marriage isn't restricted to our bodies, but also our brains.

I've discovered that couples who view pornography in marriage also train their brains to respond to images rather than to their spouse. Over time, these couples will be dismayed to find that in order to be aroused they'll need to replay the images in their mind. And if the marriage dissolves, as one woman confessed to me, their need to mentally replay the sexually stimulating images can continue into subsequent marriages regardless of how much they love or are attracted to this new person.

In general, the need for pornography is progressive. Like a drug, someone addicted to pornography will continue to need more perverse material to keep the excitement alive. It also leads to acting out sexually what's been viewed. I've heard many painful stories of people who've acted out something they've seen on a screen, only to suffer immense emotional, physical and spiritual pain, and possibly be the source of wounding to someone else.

Pornography is a great evil directed at making people sexual objects, and devaluing sex-- all part of Satan's plan. The result? Women today feel pressured to live up to the images that are now permanently imprinted in their husband's brains. Imagines of young, perfect bodies and abnormally sexualized women expressing delight at being abused and victimized in perverse and devaluing situations, set both men and women up to fail in this area. Men—because they compare their wives with the "sex bombs" on the screen and feel cheated or dissatisfied, and women who know they can never measure up to what their husbands want or seem to need them to be.

- *Does it involve anyone else?* We know that God says sex is to be exclusive between a husband and wife. Whenever we involve anyone else in the sexual relationship, God says it is prohibited. But what if that person is on a screen in your bedroom, or in your thoughts when you should be thinking about your spouse? Do you think that could also be considered involving someone else?

What is your definition of involving someone else in your marital sexual relationship? A three-some? Sexual orgies? Wife-swapping? I'm sorry for being so graphic but this is happening in marriages today, mainly because of pornography. I'm sure you'd all agree that according to God, these sexual perversions would be prohibited. But how is viewing pornography any different than these other things? Doesn't viewing pornography permanently imprint another person sexually in your brain? And if you're having sex with your spouse but you're looking at or thinking about someone else, isn't that the same as involving another in your sexual relationship? Jesus spoke out against mental sex in Matthew 5:28 when he said that adultery is more than a physical act—it is equally wrong when we do it with someone in our minds.

According to our experiment, pornography gets three strikes. First, it is clearly prohibited according to numbers 4, 7 and 9 of God's prohibition list (from Day One of this week). Second, science and personal testimony proves that pornography is extremely harmful inside and outside marriage. And third, according to Scripture viewing pornography brings someone else into your marriage bed, or future marriage bed.

- Has pornography been an issue for you in the past? In what way?

- Is it a struggle for you today? How?

- What is God asking you to do about it?

Day Four: Emotional Affairs and Masturbation

Pornography may have seemed fairly straight forward compared to what we're going to address today. Emotional affairs and masturbation are silent struggles men and women wrestle with, inside and outside marriage. And sometimes the Bible doesn't seem to have any concrete moral guidance to offer—or does it? Let's examine these two issues using our questions and find out.

Emotional Affairs

What is an emotional affair? Have you experienced one—or many? I'm convinced there are two kinds of emotional affairs. One is when someone carries on a relationship with someone in their minds. This could be someone they know well or not at all. The common characteristic of this kind of emotional affair is that the other person has no idea that they're being thought of in this way. They may think that their interaction with this person is innocent and perfectly normal, while the one imagining the affair sees their connection as intimate and proof that the other person feels the same way.

The other kind of emotional affair is when two people who are not married are carrying on an emotional relationship that would be similar to a marriage relationship, but without the physical part. Most physical affairs progress out of an emotional affair, which is why they can be so dangerous. If you're not married and your emotional connection is with another single person of the opposite sex, it could be considered good—like a close friendship that may lead to a romantic relationship. The danger for a single person comes when the emotional affair is with someone who is married, or it leads to fantasizing about having sex with them.

When I was going through my depression as a young mom, I began an emotional affair with my doctor. I began to fantasize about being with him, having sex with him, and being married to him. I made sure I always looked good when I went into his office for a visit. I imagined that he felt the same way about me. Every glance, every word, every time he put his hand on me confirmed that my feelings were justified because he felt the same way. I was wrong. His behavior towards me was nothing but innocent and normal. I was seeing it the way I wanted to—through my warped fantasy. The affair kept me from being emotionally and physically available to my husband. My love, energy and focus were on this imaginary relationship that no one knew about—or so I thought. But God knew. And you'll never guess what He did—He moved the doctor out of the country. That ended it for me. Praise God! I've since learned that what I was experiencing is called Nightingale Syndrome, a false sense of falling in love with one's medical care-taker. Maybe you've experience this too.

If we look at emotional affairs using our three questions, we'll see that God has something to say about them.

- *Are emotional affairs prohibited by God?* Go back over the prohibitions in Day One and write down your answer here:

Read over my story again. Do you see how the affair affected me? I was fantasizing about having sex with him—what does that sound like? Not only are emotional affairs prohibited based on numbers 4 (impure thoughts) and 7 (lustful passions), it is also addressed by Jesus in Matthew 5:28 under mental adultery. God is clear on this issue--having an emotional affair with someone is wrong. But you may be confused right now, especially if you're single. Earlier, I mentioned that singles having an emotional connection with another single could be something good. After all, if neither of you are married then your emotional connection would not be considered an affair. But for the single person, if you begin fantasizing about having sex with this person then you've crossed the line from something healthy to something dangerous. Now, according to Jesus in Matthew 5:28, you're committing adultery with this person. We're also not talking about a healthy emotional friendship with someone of the same sex, unless you're struggling with homosexuality and begin to fantasize about sex with that person.

We don't need to go on to the other questions at this point because we've already established that emotional affairs are wrong based on Scripture. But why are they wrong? To answer that, let's look at the other two questions. *Are they beneficial?* To validate what God says, emotional affairs weaken our resolve for sexual purity. If allowed to continue, they'll eventually lead to a physical affair—if not with the one they're having the emotional affair with, than with someone else.

Two good friends of mine both had emotional affairs with men who were unaware of what was going on. Although they didn't have a physical affair with them, they both ended up leaving their husbands for different men altogether. They destroyed their families and left their children. It all started innocently enough, so they thought, with an emotional affair.

But what if your emotional affair is with someone you're not fantasizing having sex with? Is that okay? Let's think about it. First of all, the chance of that is rare. Even so, you're still spending time, thought and energy on building an emotional connection with someone other than your spouse. How could this harm your marriage? Whatever emotional intimacy you're reserving for the other person, you're directly denying your spouse. With our expanding opportunity for social networking today through myspace and facebook, many people are reconnecting with past lovers and starting up what they think is an innocent relationship. This is a slippery slope that can lead to an affair.

Whenever we redirect our affection and attention to another we are committing adultery, God says. In fact, adultery begins long before the physical relationship begins. Adultery begins in our hearts when we redirect our affection and attention away from our spouse to someone else. We can also commit adultery against God when we redirect our affection and attention away from Him as first in our lives to someone or something else.

With regards to emotional affairs, I'm not talking about women having girlfriends and guys having male friends unless of course your friendship with them keeps you emotionally detached from your spouse.

In answer to the last question-- *"does it involve anyone else?"*--it's obvious that when you're having sex with your husband or wife and thinking about someone else, you're bringing the other person into your marriage bed—in your mind.

But is it okay if you're not married? I can answer that simply enough. If the person you're fantasizing about having sex with is not your spouse--whether you're married or not-- it's wrong based on Matthew 5:28. Jesus says to commit adultery in your mind is the same as in the flesh, and that can happen whether we're married or not. Being married or single is not the issue—being human is.

Emotional affairs have not fared well, have they? They're prohibited in Scripture, not beneficial to your marriage and involve others. Case closed.

- How have you been impacted by emotional affairs in the past?

- What about now?

- What is God showing you about your past or present emotional affairs that you've never seen before?

- What does He want you to do with what He's shown you?

Masturbation

Can you believe we're talking about masturbation in a Bible Study? If you're blushing right now, I can relate. It's definitely not your typical Bible Study topic. You may not struggle with masturbation, but you probably know someone who does. And if not an issue for you, this will help you talk to others—especially your children.

Definition: Masturbation or self-pleasuring is stimulating yourself sexually so as to reach sexual climax or release. To be clear, we're talking about self-pleasuring when alone, whether you're married or not. This does not include masturbation or mutual masturbation that occurs between a husband and wife during love-making. How does God view masturbation? Let's examine it using our three questions.

- *Is it prohibited in Scripture?* Look back over the ten prohibitions. Do you see anything that could pertain to this issue?

I've read lots of Christian books on this topic and many agree that the Bible does not speak specifically to this issue. In other words, there isn't a definite or clear "no" related to this topic. So if we can't find Scripture that prohibits masturbation, does that mean it's allowed? Let's go on to question number two.

- *Is it beneficial?* What do you think? How has masturbation benefited you, or your marriage? Or has it been harmful to you or your marriage?

Shannon Ethridge, in her book, *Every Woman's Battle,*[9] addresses the issue of masturbation. One of the myths of masturbation is that it won't hurt us, our relationship with our current or future spouse, or our relationship with God. In examining this myth, Shannon looks at issues related to masturbation that are cause for concern.

Masturbation can lead to addiction. We tend to believe that by relieving the sexual tension we feel, the need will go away. But the opposite happens. Masturbation fuels the desire rather than quenching it. The more we participate in this activity, the more we want to—then the more we *need* to.

Masturbation often involves impure thoughts or lustful passions which we already know is prohibited in Scripture. So it's clear that masturbation associated with impure thoughts is prohibited.

Masturbation can weaken your resolve for sexual purity, especially if you're single. After all, if you can't control yourself when you're alone, what makes you think you can control yourself when you're with someone else in a romantic situation?

Masturbation often continues into marriage because it trains us to self-pleasure, or as Shannon puts it, to 'fly solo' sexually. Once you've trained your body to find its own pleasure, this can cause problems if your spouse can't please you in the same way. This can be devastating in marriage. Much of the enjoyment of sex is giving pleasure to your spouse. If we feel inadequate to pleasure our spouse, it can lead to feelings of insecurity and disappointment—which diminishes the intimacy and pleasure for both.

Masturbation is one dimensional sex and is concerned with one person—us. God designed sex to be three dimensional. He planned that it would involve the whole beings of two people and that the concern of each partner would be for the other. If we're finding comfort by pleasuring ourselves, then we won't need to go to our spouse to have this need met. Instead, masturbation can keep us from experiencing true emotional intimacy inside and outside marriage. Inside marriage because we can use it to avoid physical and emotional intimacy with our spouse, and outside marriage because if it becomes addictive, we may isolate ourselves from others as the addiction and the shame from it, holds us hostage.

Then there's the issue of bonding. When we're experiencing sexual release, whatever we're looking at or thinking about becomes our trigger. But there can be additional triggers—a time of the day, a specific place, certain emotions and many others. Then when you find yourself alone, at that time of day, in that place—sexual arousal can be triggered without any provocation whatsoever.

God created sex for a husband and a wife—two people, not one. *Whenever* we take sex outside God's plan we're misusing it. And when we misuse sex it has devastating effects on us and our present or future marriage. Although the Bible does not clearly say, 'thou shalt not masturbate," God is very clear that sex is for a husband and a wife. I believe that masturbating alone is not what God wants for us sexually. However, during the sexual relationship of a husband and wife, stimulating yourself or each other is acceptable if it's something you're both comfortable with.

So how did masturbation fare? Although we don't see definite evidence against it according to God's prohibitions, we acknowledge that it's not beneficial when practiced alone, inside and outside marriage. God also warns that whenever we combine masturbation with impure or lustful thoughts it is prohibited.

My intention during this discussion is not to tell you what to do on this issue. My goal is to give you tools to help you discern before God not only this issue, but the many others you may have now or in the future. My prayer is that God will increase your wisdom and discernment as you take your personal challenges to Him using these questions as a guide.

Doing it God's way ensures that you can achieve His kind of sex—the best sex ever.

Day Five: Steps to Purity

It's hard, isn't it? While it's one thing to know what's right, it's entirely another to *do* it. I know. And so does God. Paul, in Hebrews 4:15, tells us that Jesus sympathizes with our weaknesses—He knows that we're human: *"For we do not have a high priest who is unable to sympathize with our weaknesses, but we have one who has been tempted in every way, just as we are—yet was without sin."* God understands. He knows our struggle.

- Take a moment and ask God to show you how He sympathizes with your struggle. Since God created you, He knows *you* intimately. He knows what your weaknesses are and why you fall. Ask Him to shine His light on your struggle. Write what He reveals to you here:

It's hard to imagine that Jesus was tempted in "every way" as we are, but that's what this verse says. Think about your temptations. Now try to imagine Jesus experiencing the very same ones. As you do, try to visualize His sympathy for you in each struggle. Write down what God shows you.

He also provides a way out from under the temptation. 2 Corinthians 10:13 says, *"No temptation has seized you except what is common to man. And God is faithful; he will not let you be tempted beyond what you can bear. But when you are tempted, he will also provide a way out so that you can stand up under it."*

- *"No temptation has seized you except what is common to man."* What does this phrase tell you about your struggle?

The enemy wants us to believe that we're alone in our temptation. "No one else has experienced my pain." "No one else struggles with *this.*" It's a lie. God says our struggles—whatever they may be, are common to everyone. We're never alone.

- But then the verse goes on to give us three promises. What are they?

The first is that God's faithful. It's not up for debate--it's a fact. But what is God faithful to do? He's faithful to not let us be tempted beyond what we can bear. The Bible says that we're tempted by Satan and our own evil desires. But God controls how much temptation we struggle with. And He promises that He'll never allow the temptation to be so much that it will destroy us without providing a way out so that we can remain standing. "But," I can hear you asking, "then why do I fall? Why am I still down? And why can't I get up?"

Because you didn't take His way out. He provided it, but you've yet to take it. Whenever we try to resist temptation on our own, it will overtake us--every time. Why? Because the temptation is stronger than us. God is the only One who can ensure our victory--every time.

- What temptation are you experiencing that you're not having victory over?

- What "way out" has God provided for you? What is keeping you from taking it? Maybe you've taken a piece of it, but not all of it. What is God still asking you to do in this area?

I don't know what your "way out" is, but I do know that God will not call you to handle it alone. We need each other. And He will not allow you to keep your sin a secret. Secret sins are like a poison that ripples through families, churches and communities for generations to come. The only way for some sin—especially sexual sin, to release its hold on us is when we bring it into God's redeeming light. We don't like this "way out"—but it is God's way. And remember, His ways are not our ways. Our way leads to more destruction, more temptation, and bigger secrets. God's way leads to freedom, healing and life.

Temptation always begins in the mind with a thought. God's most powerful weapon for the mind is learning to take those thoughts captive. I've talked to many Christians who believe that the thought is the sin, but really that first thought is the temptation, not the sin. It's what we do with that thought that becomes sin. If we let it in and dwell on it, it can lead to sin.

Below are three tools adapted from Shannon Ethridge's *Every Woman's Battle*[10] to help you discover God's way out for you in your particular struggle.

1. Resist

(a) *"Submit to God. Resist the devil and he will flee far from you"* (James 4:7). Submit yourself to God, James 4:7 says, and then you can resist the enemy's attacks. The first step in resisting temptation is to submit to God.

Many of us try to resist the devil before first submitting to God. As I reflect on my failures to resist temptation, I've discovered it's because I failed to submit to God first. If you've struggled with resisting temptation, then maybe you're skipping this initial step. The next time temptation comes knocking, take a moment to submit yourself and your struggle to God and ask Him for the strength to resist the enemy.

(b) "Take every thought captive." Once we submit to God, we're able to resist the enemy by taking every thought captive.

"For though we live in the world, we do not wage war as the world does. The weapons we fight with are not the weapons of the world. On the contrary, they have divine power to demolish strongholds. We demolish arguments and every pretension that sets itself up against the knowledge of God, and we take captive every thought to make it obedient to Christ" (2 Corinthians 10:3-5).

Taking every thought captive takes practice. The more often you do it the easier it gets. Whenever I get a thought that I know is not from God, I stop the thought at the imaginary door to my brain. Immediately I pray and ask God to take this thought captive. I give it to Him and ask Him to replace this thought with His truth. It works for all kinds of thoughts-- an impure thought, a jealous thought, selfish thought, etc.

Once again, the thought is not the sin--what we do with it is. However, there may be things we're doing which feed those thoughts that actually *are* sin. Therefore, we need a plan to redirect our thoughts and actions so we can avoid the temptation in the first place.

- How do you take a thought captive? Give an example of when you've taken a thought captive.

2. Redirect

What are you doing, reading or watching that may be feeding your tempting thoughts? Are there places you're going, people you're seeing, activities you're involving yourself in that are weakening your ability to stand up under temptation? Ask God to show you what triggers tempting thoughts for you. Make a plan to change your lifestyle or circumstances, so that you can begin to have victory in this area.

(a) Have a plan. What are you going to do the next time temptation arises? With sexual temptation we'll usually have people, places or images that trigger arousal. Unless you're married and it's your spouse you're having sexual thoughts about, have a plan to change your surroundings or redirect what you're doing if you find unwanted sexual thoughts invading

your mind. Turn off what you're watching, switch to a new book. If you're sitting, go for a walk. If you're lying down, get up. Ask God to give you specific things you can do to redirect your thoughts and actions the next time sexual temptation threatens to defeat you.

Most importantly, have one or more friends you can call who will support you, pray for you and hold you accountable whenever you need them—yes, even at midnight.

(b) Do the next thing you were going to do. Often we'll be in the middle of something when a tempting thought comes, and then before we know it we're distracted from what we are supposed to be doing. Instead, take that thought captive and then keep doing what you were doing. Or go on to something you should be doing. Get back to work, make dinner for your family, read to your child. Pray.

But none of these points will help unless this next one is an ongoing pursuit--renewing your mind.

3. Renew

(a) Read God's word daily. Even if it doesn't seem like you're absorbing the verses, because you've placed them in your mind and meditated on them with your heart, the Holy Spirit now has them available to remind you of the next time a tempting thought arises. When you ask God to take a tempting thought captive, the Holy Spirit can replace it with a verse or thought you've already learned.

(b) Get an anchor verse. Memorize a verse that you can recite out loud when temptation comes. A good one is 2 Corinthians 10:3-5.

(c) *Read Christian books.* I find that God often uses Christian books to reinforce what He's teaching me in His word. I'm always amazed when my daily Scripture verse is reiterated in a Christian resource I'm currently reading. Henry Blackaby, in *Experiencing God,*[11] says that God speaks to us through prayer, His Word and the church (other believers) to reveal to us His ways, His truth, His purposes and His plans. Through great Christian books, God will use what He's shown other believers to teach you.

(d) Most importantly…pray, pray, pray. Pray before the tempting thought comes, pray when you get it, pray after it's gone—just keep praying. The power of pray over the enemy's schemes to tempt us is the foundation of all these tools. They won't work unless we call down the power of God into our situation to make them work for us. This is the "way out" God has provided—and prayer infuses His power into His "way out," allowing us the sweet victory of standing up under the temptation (1 Corinthians 10:13).

Last but not least, remember that God loves you just as you are--all messed up. If going through this week has left you feeling full of shame, that's not from God. God is not our condemner. He is the one who comes to rescue us, set us free from that which has a hold on us, and give us the hope and strength we desperately need to fight against the temptations that threaten to destroy us. When you're drowning in shame, *run* to God—He's waiting to *lift you up* and give you peace.

Think About It...

- What's the most significant truth you've learned this week? Write out the verse (if applicable) that God used to speak to you.

- What is God asking you to do with this new truth?

- Write out your response (prayer) to God here:

CHAPTER FIVE

Trusting God

Day One: How Well Do You Know God?

"I keep asking that the God of our Lord Jesus Christ, the glorious Father may give you the Spirit of wisdom and revelation, so that you may know Him better" (Ephesians 1:17).

How well do you know God? Do you even want to know Him better? The way you perceive God's character may determine if He is someone you even care to know. Regardless of what you've believed in the past about God, I pray that Chapter One has helped you discover who God really is. If you have begun to put some of the steps into place from Chapter Two, then you may actually be developing true intimacy with Him. This is the first step in transitioning from knowing *of* God to really *knowing* Him.

I have good news. Whether you want to know God or not—He wants to know you. Look at the verse at the top of the page.

- Who is responsible for us knowing God?

- Who teaches us about God?

- What gives you the idea from this verse that God really wants you to know Him?

So, how *is* your relationship with God? Let me compare how we grow in our relationship with God to how we grow in our relationship with other people by using the five Levels of Intimacy mentioned in Chapter Four of *The Invisible Bond,* and Chapter Four in *Kiss Me Again.* The chart below uses the levels of intimacy in relationships with others and adapts it to our relationship with God.

				LEVELS OF INTIMACY				

LEVELS OF INTIMACY

Lowest Level — Know of God	Low Level — Learning about God from others	Moderate Level — Begin a relationship with God Begin to Know God—limited intimacy	High Level — Sharing more of ourselves with God: feelings, desires, and struggles	Highest Level — Completely surrendered to God Able to have complete openness and honesty about everything with Him--our shameful past, doubts, fears, hopes, etc.

The first thing I want you to grasp is that God knows each of us at the highest level of intimacy. He knows us better than we know ourselves.

- Read Psalm 139:1-10. Write down all the ways God knows you.

This is true intimacy. Even if you haven't given God a moment's thought your whole life, He already knows you completely. Does that alarm you? It needn't. The amazing story of the gospel is that even when God knew every last shameful secret, and before we had the slightest thought of Him, He wanted to have a relationship with us at the highest level of intimacy.

I often ask God, "With all you know about me, why would you want a relationship with me?" I won't completely understand until I see Him face to face, but for now I believe Him when He says that before He created me He already loved me. It has nothing to do with who I am, how I think, or what I've done. It's because of who *He* is. He loves me because He chooses to, not because I've earned it.

- Which of the above levels of intimacy are you at in your relationship with God?

If you've asked Jesus to forgive your sins and come in and take control of your life, then you have positioned yourself on the path to all we've talked about in this study--complete forgiveness and healing. If you've never asked Christ into your life and given Him complete control, go back to Chapter One, lesson two and follow the prayer to receive Jesus Christ as your personal Savior.

Have you moved beyond the moderate level? Then you've truly begun to know God. You are becoming deeply intimate with the God of the universe. The extent of the depth of this incredible intimacy will be directly proportional to how humble and broken you're willing to be. God says in James 4:10 that when we "humble ourselves before Him, He will lift us up." The more we humble ourselves, ironically, the more God "lifts us up" closer to Him.

- Now that you've recognized the level of intimacy you're at with God, what's keeping you from moving to the next level?

If you don't know, ask God—because He does. Maybe there's something God is asking you to do, or not do, that you're ignoring. Humility without obedience is a waste. If you don't obey, you get stuck, and you can't move on. If you've been stalled at a certain level with God for a long time, check with Him to see what's causing the hold up. Then do something about it right away. I'm confident regardless of how difficult the request seems you'll be pleased with the results.

Day Two: Why I Can Trust Him

"Do you want to get well?" Jesus asked this question to a man who for thirty-eight years had been an invalid. What a great question! Have you ever thought about the answer? Many of us are invalids because of our pasts. We're sick, injured or handicapped by the pain and shame of our past, but it doesn't mean we all want to get well.

- Read John 5:1-9. What are the three conditions of the people who are described as disabled?

- If you look at the three conditions from a spiritual, emotional or mental perspective, which one would you use to describe yourself right now?

- What answer does the man give Jesus when He asks him if he wants to get well?

- Can you read between the lines? Who is he saying is at fault for his continued disabled condition?

- What does the man trust in to heal him?

- What about you? Do you want to get well? Why or why not?

- If the answer is yes, what or who are you trusting in to heal you?

When we've been hurt sexually our ability to trust is greatly compromised. Whether we were betrayed sexually as a child by a family member or trusted friend, raped by a stranger or someone we knew, or used and discarded by someone we thought loved us as a teenager or adult, trust is the first thing to die in us. It's a matter of survival. When we trust and then get hurt, rejected or abandoned, everything in us screams to protect ourselves from it ever happening again. But painfully, it does happen again and again. And with each person, with every disappointment, the glimmer of trust flickering in our soul slowly dies--even our trust in God--until you feel like the man at the pool, a wounded invalid, alone, abandoned, with no one to help, no one to trust.

But it's a lie. Its all part of the enemy's shrewd plan. The wounding from our pasts keeps us isolated from God and others so that we can never heal, never find freedom, never have hope. The lie convinces us that if we can't trust people who we can see, then we certainly can't trust a God who we can't see.

Do you want to get well? Then you'll have to trust God. Not sure if you can—or if you even want to? Well let me ask you this: how is trying to get well on your own working for you? I'm going to assume if you're going through this study the answer is, "not too well." I know because I've been there too. Until I met the One I could trust to make me well and set me free. Let me introduce Him to you.

- What about God is trustworthy?

2 Samuel 7:28

Psalm 13:5

Psalm 19:7

Psalm 33:21

Psalm 111:7

Psalm 119:86

- Look back over your answers. Which trustworthy character of God is the most significant for you?

- Which one is the hardest for you to trust in? Why?

- What are some benefits of trusting God? Read the following verses to answer the question.

1 Chronicles 5:20

Psalm 22:4-5

Psalm 37:5-6

Psalm 40:4

Psalm 56:3-4

Psalm 78:22

Psalm 125:1

Proverbs 3:5-6

Isaiah 12:2

Isaiah 25:9

Isaiah 30:15

Nahum 1:7

- What have you been missing out on because you were afraid to trust God with your past, present or future?

Day Three: Counterfeit Trust

If you're having trouble trusting God with your past, you're not alone. I understand that struggle. One of the questions I often get is, "Why would God allow me to go through what I did?" Women who have been sexually abused or raped wrestle over this nagging thought. "Where was God?" "If He loved me, why didn't He protect me?" Or maybe like me you're wondering why God allowed you to make some of the choices you made, especially when He knew your heart to follow Him. Regardless of what happened in your past, or what your unspoken doubts are, God has answers to all your questions. He knows and cares. He wants you to know the truth about Him and the truth about what happened in your past.

When I began to implore God with my nagging doubts, He was quick to reassure me of His constant presence—even when I was unaware of it. God was always there, cautioning me about the danger of my choices—I just wasn't listening. However, this can be a more difficult concept for victims of sexual abuse or rape because, you had no choice. Where was God then?

Right beside you. I know that's hard to believe. If God was there—if He could see—why didn't He stop it? Dan Allender, in *The Wounded Heart,* says that trusting God is one of the

74

most damaging consequences of sexual abuse. "Where was God? Does He love me? Can I trust Him? If I can, what am I to trust Him for?"[12] are some of the questions an abuse victim will ask, Allendar says.

And the result? "The devilishness of abuse," says Allender, "is that it does Satan's work of deceiving children about God's true nature and encouraging them to mistrust Him. Fearing to trust God, the abuse victim will naturally choose other gods to provide her (him) with life, whether alcohol, promiscuity, or approval-seeking." [13]

But I have good news for you—God is not afraid of our questions, doubts, mistrust, even our anger. Allendar says, "Those who trust God most are those whose faith permits them to risk wrestling with Him over the deepest questions of life. Good hearts are captured in a divine wrestling match; fearful, doubting hearts stay clear of the mat."[14]

All I can say is that for whatever reason, God has allowed us to have free will. Although the severity of the actions vary, sometimes our free will is a source of pain to others—they're the victim, we're the perpetrator. Other times we're the victim--at the whim of another's free will. But with absolute certainty I can assure you that God sees the plight of the victim. He hears our cry and promises--guarantees-- that He will defend our cause. He *will* make it right. *He* will, not us. He will only work when we stop trying to do it on our own.

This issue of trusting God is not reserved for the sexual abuse victim. We all struggle with it. It is the condition of the human heart. It's not a question of do we trust or not trust—but what we trust in. We all trust in something—if it's not God then it *is* someone or something else. Allender sums it up by saying, "When we fail to trust the real God, we do not escape trusting someone or something. We cannot fail to trust God without turning our trust to something that becomes a new god for us." [15]

- What or who do you trust in? Read the following verses and write down what we choose to trust in rather than God. Ask God to show you which ones you're trusting in.

Psalm 20:7-8

Psalm 49:6

Psalm 49:13-14

Psalm 118:8-9

Isaiah 47:10

Jeremiah 7:4

Jeremiah 13:25

Jeremiah 48:7

Ezekiel 16:15

If you're a sexual abuse survivor and haven't had any counseling or been through a support group with other survivors, then I encourage you to get Dan Allender's book, *The Wounded Heart*. There's also an accompanying workbook that would be worthwhile in your healing process. In the studies I lead, we insist that survivors of childhood sexual abuse go through some counseling or participate in a support group for sexual abuse before they come into our study. By dealing with the pain of the abuse first, they are more prepared to honestly engage in this study and explore the destructive sexual choices that they made subsequent to the abuse.

Day Four: Coping Mechanisms – Self-Medicating the Pain

You may not feel it, but you're in pain. If you've had sexual wounding in your past, by someone else or your own choices, pain and shame have become your unwelcome companions. First Corinthians 6:18 says that sexual sin is not like other sins—it's the one sin that we commit against our own bodies. In Chapter Five of the *Invisible Bond*, I share how the wounding of sex is not just physical, but emotional, mental and spiritual as well. So believe it or not, you're in pain somewhere--your body, your emotions, your mind or your spirit. Most likely, in all of them. Still skeptical? The fact that you're going through this study is one good indication. You may not recognize the pain—but you're feeling it.

Another reason you may not feel the pain is because you've succeeded at masking it. We all have little habits, comforts, or distractions to help us cope with unwanted thoughts, feelings, and fears. For many of us, the coping mechanism isn't a problem--we think. At least it's not taking over our lives. We're still managing, coping, surviving. That's good, you reason. Until you discover that you're still dealing with the same struggles, issues and addictions as last year, and the year before that. Actually—you're stuck. You may be surviving, but you're not thriving.

Most of us don't recognize that we are using coping mechanisms, or that we're even in pain, until we ask God to show us. Today is your day to ask. It may take more than one day to fully discover your particular medication of choice. As you proceed, do so prayerfully. You may want to say this prayer to God:

"Lord, shine your light on my pain. Reveal to me what I use to cope with my pain instead of trusting in you."

What is a Coping Mechanism?

A coping mechanism is anything we use to control, deny, escape or self-medicate our feelings instead of bringing them to God. Things such as a time of day, situation, place or person can trigger the painful emotion that compels us to resort to our coping mechanism. The following chart lists some examples of coping mechanisms. Very likely you'll find yours in this list. But you may have one that isn't included. If so, add it in.

How Do We Identify a Coping Mechanism?

Sometimes a coping mechanism is so ingrained in our daily lives we don't recognize its presence or purpose. It seemingly becomes a part of who we believe we are. Often the activity we use is not necessarily wrong, but we will use it excessively or participate in it when we should be doing something else—like caring for our family, working, spending time with God, etc.

Using the following verse and chart below, ask God to reveal your particular coping mechanisms. Ask God to show you what triggers your coping mechanism—is it a time of day, an activity, certain people, certain emotions? Make sure you write those down to help you understand what puts you in a vulnerable position.

Coping Mechanism	Trigger (Situation/Emotion)	Time of Day	Replacement Activity
"Search me O God, and know my heart; test me and know my anxious thoughts. See if there is any offensive way in me, and lead me in the way everlasting" (Psalm 139:23-24).			
More Obvious			
Alcohol			
Drugs (legal/illegal)			
Sexual Affair/Promiscuity			
Eating Disorders			
Smoking			
Less Obvious			
Emotional Affairs/Fantasizing			
Shopping			
Overeating			
Hypercritical			
Too much time on phone			
Over commitment to work or church service			
Perfectionism			
Computer Games			
Internet, Chat Rooms, Email			
Television			
Gossip			
Anger, nag or berate husband/children			
Emotionally withdrawn			
Other:			

The Danger of Coping Mechanisms

Why is identifying your coping mechanism so crucial? Because it masks your emotional pain. When you ignore the pain, you don't heal. Imagine you are visiting the doctor with a particular pain in a specific area of your body, but before you see him you take some pain medication. Now the pain is gone. When you try to explain to the doctor where it hurts, you are unable to give him the information he needs to properly diagnosis you. He'll want to see you when you are experiencing the pain in order to fully appreciate what you will need for treatment.

The same thing happens with our emotional and spiritual pain. If we dull it with a coping mechanism we won't feel it—and we won't bring it to God for healing. Obviously, He knows where it hurts, and what we need for healing—but if we're not in pain we won't ask for help.

Replacing Your Coping Mechanism

You can't just eliminate your coping mechanism without replacing it with something healthy. Because of our self-protective nature that likes to avoid pain, without a plan to replace your existing method, you'll just substitute it with something else—maybe less dangerous, but just as destructive.

First, commit to replacing your existing mechanism with something healthy. Here are some examples:

- Pray

- Meditate on God's Word

- Journal or write a letter to God

- Go for a walk, or exercise

- Do the activity you should be doing (i.e., working, household chores, spending time with your children, spouse, going to bed earlier, etc.)

- Read a good book

- Your great idea here!

Write down your plan—pray over it. Ask God to help you recognize when you're experiencing the pain, shame or fear and give you the courage to reach for the choice that will allow you to trust God instead. Every time you embrace your pain and choose a godly replacement, you defeat its hold on you one more time. Eventually that struggle will hardly come knocking at all.

Day Five: Trusting in the Unseen

Why is it so hard to trust God? We want to—we try. But for many of us the results are less than fruitful. The experience can be extremely frustrating, even scary. And so we're left with what we know and can do—we trust ourselves.

I pray that throughout this week you have learned what or who it is you're trusting in instead of God. But even more, I pray that you are willing to lay your counterfeit down so you can trust in someone who's for real and for sure—God.

Once more, read the following verses, but this time I want you to focus on what the verse says should be the object of your trust and what result it brings.

Psalm 13:5

Psalm 20:7-8

Proverbs 3:5-6

- In contrast, what happens when we trust in the things of this world?

Psalm 20:7-8

Psalm 146:3-4

Proverbs 11:28

Isaiah 47:10-11

Now that you recognize your need to trust God, you may be wondering, "How much trust or faith do I need?" Great question. The answer may surprise you.

Not very much. In fact—only a little.

- Read Luke 17:5-6. What did the disciples ask Jesus to do for them?

- What was His response?

Jesus says we only need faith as small as a mustard seed. Just how small is a mustard seed? Well at the time, it was the smallest known seed in the Middle East. But the size of the mustard seed isn't the issue. What Jesus was really saying was that the size of your faith doesn't matter—even a little tiny bit of faith will do. Why is that?

Because the quantity of the faith isn't as important as the object of the faith. In other words, if the object of our faith is big enough, then the amount of our faith is insignificant. Charles Price, in *Stop Trying to Live For Jesus...Let Him Live Through You,* says, "The all-important thing is not the quantity of our faith, but the quality of the object in which our faith is placed. ...Small faith in a strong object will still enable that object to work."[16] Price goes on to give a great example to illustrate. He tells of a time when he flew on an airplane seated between two other passengers. Each one of them had different quantities of faith in the ability of the airplane to transport them safely to their destination.

"...The three of us in that row each had a different quantity of faith. The woman had only a mustard-seed-sized faith. She had just enough to allow herself to be persuaded to make the journey. I, however, was a little more confident and had potato-sized faith. The man on my right probably never even thought about there being any possibility of his not arriving safely as he bounded on board with his melon-sized faith. But the remarkable thing was this: although the woman had only mustard-seed-sized faith and I had potato-sized faith and the man had melon-sized faith, we all arrived at our destination at the same time. The all important thing was not the quantity of our faith but the object in which we placed our faith."[17]

You just need a little faith to trust God with your pain and shame, hurts and wounds. God is bigger than enough. Whatever faith you lack, God makes up, because He can and He will. But I promise you, as you trust in God and find Him faithful, your faith will increase naturally. Just like the airplane illustration, mustard-sized faith grows to potato-sized faith and then to melon-sized faith before you know it.

It just takes practice.

Think About It…

- What's the most significant truth you've learned this week? Write out the verse (if applicable) that God used to speak to you.

- What is God asking you to do with this new truth?

- Write out your response (prayer) to God here.

CHAPTER SIX

The Bonding of Sex

Day One: God's Purpose for Sex

Have you ever wondered what God thinks of sex? After all, sex was His idea. After God finished creating man and woman—the grand finale of His magnificent handiwork, He gave His first command to the man and the woman in Genesis 1:28: "Be fruitful and increase in number; fill the earth and subdue it." In others words, have sex—lots of sex--and fill the earth with people. More people—more sex…you get the picture. Then in Genesis 1:31, God gives us His evaluation of all that He's made—including sex: "God saw all that He had made, and it was very good."

God says sex is "very good." Would you agree? If sex in your experience has been a source of pain and wounding, you may disagree. You may be afraid of sex, dislike sex, or have no desire for sex. If so, then I'm glad you're working through this study. For many years in my marriage I didn't consider sex good either. I lacked desire, struggled initiating or participating in it, and seldom enjoyed it--until God broke the negative bonds to my past and aligned my lies about sex with His truth. The result? Did it really make a difference? Just ask my husband. Not only do I desire it more, I enjoy it. Rather than being a passive observer, now I'm an active participant—much to my husband's delight. And God's too.

Married or single, if you can't view sex as "very good" then I pray God will heal your pain, expose the lies and change your mind about sex. By the end of this study I hope you can join me and God in declaring, "Sex is *good!*"

God had a lot in mind when He created sex. It wasn't just to make babies and give us pleasure—although these are two very good reasons. From Linda Dillow and Lorraine Pintus's book, *Intimate Issues*,[18] let's explore some of the incredible benefits God provides husbands and wives in a sexual relationship. (You'll also find this list and my own descriptions of each in Chapter Nine of *Kiss Me Again).*

- *God gave the gift of sex to create life.* How does this benefit of sex glorify God and enhance a marriage relationship? Why is a marriage relationship the best place to raise children?

- *God gave the gift of sex for intimate oneness.* Read Genesis 2:24. After reading this verse and Chapter Two in *The Invisible Bond*, how would you describe this "oneness?"

- *God gave the gift of sex for knowledge.* Read Genesis 4:1. The Hebrew word for sexual intercourse is *yadah,* which means to know. When we have sex with our spouse, we know them at the deepest, most intimate level--physically, spiritually and emotionally. Think about those you've had sex with in your past. Knowing someone intimately inside marriage is a gift. Outside marriage, it becomes a liability. How has your intimate knowledge of others affected you today? Your marriage?

- *God gave the gift of sex for pleasure.* God is serious about sex being pleasurable for both the man and the woman. He gave one or two verses to describe the oneness of sex, and the intimate knowledge sex provides, but an entire book on the pleasure of sex. Chapter Ten of this study will be devoted to The Song of Songs--God's book on sex. Careful--it might make you blush.

- Read Proverbs 5:15-19. Is the thought of sex pleasurable to you? Why or why not?

I talk to many women who don't experience sexual pleasure—for a variety of reasons. For some, the sex they experienced before marriage left them feeling used, vulnerable or humiliated. Those emotions can follow us into marriage. Maybe sex reminds you of the shame and guilt of past sexual choices. You can't help associating sex with something sinful or dirty. For those who've been abused or raped, your experience has been traumatic, even violent. Sex for you is fearful, distasteful, and probably painful. But for all of us, past sexual experiences can keep us from trusting—God, ourselves and our spouses. The past creeps into the present, sabotaging the relationship and poisoning our marriage beds.

Are you one of the many I've talked to who has yet to experience an orgasm—that "wow" of sex I talk about in Chapter Three in *The Invisible Bond* or Chapter Two in *Kiss Me Again?* The chemicals and hormones we release during sex give us that pleasurable feeling. If you're married and still missing out on this important piece of the pleasure God has for you, I encourage you to get some Christian books on the art of sex. I know what you're thinking. Sex is sex—we'll figure it out. Yes, of course, we can figure it out, but there's always room for improvement.

It's okay to learn from others in this area. Why not glean from those who have figured out how to do it really well. If sex is okay for you but you're looking for "very good" sex, pick up a copy of *The Act of Marriage* by Tim LeHaye, or *The Married Guy's Guide to Great Sex* by Chris and Joy Penner. My husband and I have benefited from both of these great Christian resources. Read them together. Then have sex. Find out what God has in mind when it comes to the pleasure of sex.

- *God gave the gift of sex as a defense against temptation.* Read 1 Corinthians 7:2-5. Why does God encourage us not to deprive each other of sexual fulfillment?

- How does having our sexual desires met in marriage keep us from temptation?

I remember when my husband and I fasted from sex for a month. Some interesting things happened to us. First, our desire for sex increased. We thought about sex more, talked about sex more and definitely wanted it more. Secondly, my husband noticed about three weeks into the fast that he began to experience some temptation sexually. It was subtle at first, but he began noticing other women throughout his day, unlike before. It was good that we only had one more week to go. And I learned a valuable lesson. I was instrumental in helping guard my husband from sexual temptation, and in keeping his eyes only for me.

- *God gave the gift of sex for comfort.* Did you know that we can comfort our spouse with sex? Read 2 Samuel 12:24. Why did Bathsheba need comforting?

- How does sex provide comfort for us?

There was a time in our marriage when I allowed my husband to comfort me using sex. At the time, I was going through a serious depression. I had no desire for sex. Eric, feeling helpless, expressed his desire to comfort me sexually. I made a decision to submit to him whenever he wanted to have sex, even though I had no desire. Now when I look back on that time, guess what I remember? Not the months of sadness and pain I experienced, but the sweet times of Eric expressing comfort to me through sex. I believe now that Eric played a significant part in my healing. You see, not only do those chemicals we release give us pleasure, they also reduce pain and allow healing to happen. God allowed sex to play a significant role in my healing.

- How has your view of sex changed now that you know the many benefits God provides through sex?

Day Two: Sex is Intensely Bonding

No wonder God makes sex intensely bonding. In order to accomplish all His amazing purposes for sex, it has to be. But when we misuse sex, this intense bond is why it's so wounding as well. Today we're going to look specifically at the bonding nature of sex. In preparation, please read Chapter Two in the companion book, *The Invisible Bond: how to break free from your sexual past.*

Read Mark 10:7-9 and 1 Corinthians 6:16.

The phrase, "two will become one flesh" is used in both verses and means the same thing. If you're married now or have been in the past, spend a moment remembering all the details of your wedding day. Walking down the aisle, the ceremony, the vows, the reception. Quite a day of memory, isn't it? Now imagine that you're a bride or groom during early Bible times. There's no white dress, no journey down an aisle—no formal "I do." Guess what your marriage ceremony is? *Sex.* That's it—you're married now.

- The *marriage license* does not create the bond—sex does. How does this make you feel about your past sexual relationships?

- If sex is the marriage ceremony—and the break-up a divorce, how many marriages and divorces have you had sexually?

- How do you feel, knowing that whether it was a one night stand or a marriage commitment you've created the same bond?

This would be a good time to ask how your sexual history list is coming along. I understand if you've avoided it. It's very painful, acknowledging the truth about our pasts. If you haven't started, I encourage you to start today. If you've already started, take some time today to ask God if there's anything else you're missing. Trust me in this. Even if you feel it's all done. God had me add things to my list that I wouldn't have considered sex. And I would have missed out on complete healing if I hadn't given Him another opportunity to search my heart.

- Imagine the hearts in Chapter Two of *The Invisible Bond*. Parts of each one are left on the other. Now think about your past sexual experiences. What did you leave behind with each partner?

- What did you take with you from each partner in your past?

- Take a moment and pray. What does God want to restore in you that was taken?

- What does He want to remove that you've brought with you?

- Spend some time in prayer right now. Give God time to show you the truth about your past. Ask Him:

  - *To reveal more of your sexual history list.*

  - *To show you what has been stripped away from you because of bonds to past sexual partners.*

  - *To show you how being attached to others is holding you back from being all that God wants you to be.*

Remember to review the chapter on coping mechanisms if this exercise triggers emotions that cause you pain. Have your strategy plan ready. God will bless you as you persevere.

Day Three: Sex is Holy

Sex is *holy*. Say it out loud a couple of times to let it sink in. You may find this difficult to comprehend, just as I once did. I had a lot of names for sex—but holy never crossed my lips, until God revealed to me how spiritual, divine and glorifying to Him marital sex could be. This was undoubtedly the most significant, life-changing, mind-transforming truth I learned about sex.

In his book, *Restoring Sexual Sanity*,[19] Randy Alcorn talks about how God designed the sexual union to be a truly intimate experience. The primary word used in the Old Testament for sexual intercourse is *yadah*, which means "to know," as in Genesis 4:1 which says, "Now Adam *knew* Eve his wife and she conceived and bore Cain." (KJV) The kind of intimacy characterized by *yadah* is not a distant, merely factual knowledge, but a personal, intimate and experiential knowledge by one person of another.

- In Daniel 11:32 we read: "…the people who *know* their God." What similarity could there be between *know/knew* in Genesis 4:1 and Daniel 11:32?

The words "knew" and "know" come from the same Hebrew word—*yadah*. Are you amazed? I am. God uses a word that means sexual intercourse to describe a believer's relationship with God. Alcorn says, "To know one's marriage partner in the act of sex is analogous to developing intimacy with God."[20] In sexual intercourse, God has given us a living picture illustrating what it means to be one with Him. This is one reason that sex is *holy*.

Is this a new concept for you? It was for me. But then I realized that my view of sex and God's view of sex weren't the same. And God's view wasn't the one that needed to change. Our culture's understanding of sex has become so perverted that it's hard for us to imagine it being holy. But we return to the holiness of sex when we realize that God used it to shed light on the greatest intimate relationship ever known—our relationship with Him.

- Do you have a hard time thinking of sex as holy? Why or Why not?

- How have your past sexual experiences impacted your attitude towards sex?

- The enemy has set us up to fail in the area of sex for a specific purpose. What is that purpose?

- How has he used sex against you?

How could something that God created as holy, pure, and precious become so shameful, cheap, and misused? Satan took what God designed for our good and used it against us. Because sex involves the whole person—spirit, emotions, mind, and body—its abuse causes comprehensive damage. But the greatest impact of sexual sin is relational.

What a shrewd plan. What better way to keep people from drawing closer to God than to keep them from trusting people? And if I can't trust you, whom I see, then I most certainly can't trust a God that I can't see.

How has God changed your mind about sex today?

Day Four: The Science of Sex

"I praise you because I am fearfully and wonderfully made, your works are wonderful, I know that full well" (Psalm 139:14).

I'm excited. I *love* this part. When I was growing up, I knew God said to save sex for marriage—but I didn't know why. When I learned about the brain and sex, I was overwhelmed by God's amazing plan and purpose for us sexually. And for the first time, I knew why God wanted us to wait.

Exciting research on the brain and sex has revealed that men and women release powerful chemicals and hormones that create a unique bond with each other—a superglue, one flesh bond. The hormone especially significant is oxytocin, which researchers call the 'love' hormone. Preliminary research reveals the fascinating role oxytocin plays in the bonding of human relationships.

When we save sex for the one we marry, this is the only person we create a chemical bond with. But if we've had sex with others, whether through abuse or our own choices, we create this same bond, impacting our ability to have the kind of bond God designed for us in marriage. In fact, we bring each past sexual partner with us, chemically, spiritually and emotionally into the next relationship, and finally into our marriage. These past bonds keep us tied to the past, and unable to bond in the future. Research indicates that we release less oxytocin with each subsequent sexual partner, thereby inhibiting our ability to bond in successive relationships. This is why we need to heal from our past bonds, and let God sever the one-flesh bond we've created with all past partners.

For a greater understanding of this exciting research and how past bonding hurts us in the future, read Chapter Three in *The Invisible Bond: how to break free from your sexual past,* or Chapter Two in *Kiss Me Again: Restoring Lost Intimacy in Marriage.*

- After you've finished reading one of these chapters, write down in your own words as well as you can what happens to our brains when we have sex.

- What do you find encouraging about this information? Why?

- What do you find discouraging about this information? Why?

When I first learned this, I was encouraged and discouraged at the same time. Can you relate? First I was encouraged that science backed up what God had been saying from the beginning of creation. God has a good, loving reason for us to save sex for marriage. He's not trying to spoil our fun or cause us unnecessary sexual frustration. Not only does He want to provide a means for us to create a life-time bond that will enhance us personally and in marriage, but He also wants to protect us from the damaging consequences of creating multiple bonds outside marriage.

But I was also discouraged—worried actually. Because now I realized that all those sexual bonds I'd created outside marriage had deprived me of the oxytocin I needed to create the kind of bond I wanted with my present husband. Are you feeling the same? A little oxytocin-deprived? Thankfully God didn't leave me in despair. I've since learned that God doesn't reveal anything that He isn't willing and able to deliver us from or restore to us—even something as nebulous as oxytocin.

- Read Joel 2:25. Write out the verse here:

- Read Exodus 10:12-15. Why did God send the locusts to Egypt? What did the locusts do?

God sent the locusts to show His glory and power to Pharaoh, the Egyptians and the Israelites. It was also a consequence to Pharaoh for not listening and obeying God.

- Read Amos 4:9. Who did God send the locusts to this time and why?

First God sent the locusts to protect His people, the Israelites, from the Egyptians, but now He is sending them to His *own* people. Sounds like tough love, doesn't it? Why would God allow something so destructive to happen to the people He loved? When we go our own way we will suffer consequences for our actions. God will use those consequences to cause us pain. The pain drives us back to Him. If you're a parent you've used the same strategy to remind your children that obeying you is their best choice in order to avoid consequences.

God was reminding the Israelites of His Sovereignty and great power. Just like He used the locusts and other plagues to turn Pharaoh's heart to obedience, He used them to turn the Israelites hearts back to Him.

- What are some consequences you've experienced because of your past sexual choices?

If you were a victim of someone else's sexual sin, what you're feeling is not a consequence of your sin because you didn't do anything wrong. Instead, you're experiencing the consequence of someone's sin against you.

- What consequences are you experiencing because of someone else's sin?

Whether the consequences are from your own sin or someone else's, God will use the resulting pain to drive you to a deeper relationship with Him. When you respond to God's leading you'll discover Him in a whole new way. And He will turn your pain into something beautiful—it's true. You may even exclaim, as I and so many others have, "Thank you Lord for the pain that drew me closer to you and changed my life forever!"

The locusts swarmed in to devour and destroy their crops, trees and everything green. Imagine with me that sexual bonding outside marriage (whether by choice or force) is the locust and our brain is what has been destroyed.

- What do you feel has been devoured or destroyed in you because of your sexual past? Do you believe God can restore what's been taken?

- Read Joel 2:25 again. What does God say He'll do?

- I imagine if locusts ate everything it would take some years for the crops and trees to grow back to the same level of production. How many years have you lost because of your sexual past? Do you believe God can restore all that's been taken from you?

I love the visual of crops. When they'd been restored to their growing and producing potential, no one looking at them would have known what they'd been through. In other words, they were restored as if nothing had been taken.

- Do you believe God can restore what the enemy has robbed from you as if it were never taken?

- What would you like God to restore to you?

Day Five: The Impact of Sexual Bonding

You've had sex, but now sex has *you*. A sobering reality. What we'd give to relive the earlier years with wisdom and foresight—knowing that *all* our choices impact our future, negatively as well as positively. One of the ways sex can impact relationships outside marriage is by inhibiting emotional growth. Wherever we're at emotionally when we begin to have sex outside marriage, is where our emotional intimacy can stall. We feel close, but the bonding from sex can give us a false sense of intimacy, making us feel closer than we actually are. Then if we marry, we soon discover that we don't know each other as well as we thought we did, causing conflict and dissension to surface.

To prepare for today's lesson, please read about the five levels of emotional intimacy and how sex outside marriage impacts emotional growth from Chapter Four in *The Invisible Bond,* or Chapter Four in *Kiss Me Again.*

Did you notice something familiar as you read about the levels of intimacy? Back in chapter five of this study we used those same levels to examine our relationship with God. The same is true of human relationships, with one exception. In our relationship with God, He's already at the highest level with us and we are moving up the levels towards Him. In our human relationships we need to progress together through the levels in order to have true intimacy.

- Make a list of some of your relationships. What level are you at with each?

- If you're married, and had sex before marriage—what level were you at?

- At what level of emotional intimacy are you and your spouse communicating today?

- What does your pre-marital sex have to do with where you are today emotionally?

- Is God calling you to fast from sex with your spouse? For how long? Before you implement this, ask God to confirm it through prayer, His word and your spouse.

Maybe you didn't have sex with your present spouse before marriage, but had sex with others in previous relationships. The negative associations of those sexual bonds could be impacting your ability to risk true emotional intimacy in your marriage. Your past wounds may be keeping you from risking emotional intimacy in the present. Ask God to reveal anything from your past that is impacting you today. Use the following space to write down whatever He says to you:

- Whether you're married or single, think about your past romantic relationships. What level did you start having sex in any or all of your relationships?

- What impact did the early debut of sex have on the break-up of your relationships?

- If single, how do you think your past sexual experiences are impacting your choices in romantic partners today? For example, do you find yourself attached to partners you know are not good for you—ones that are emotionally, sexually or physically abusive? Or do you tend to break up but then find yourself going back to the same person over and over?

Sexual bonding doesn't just impact our emotions and relationships, it also impacts our thoughts and attitudes towards sex. In Chapter Four of *The Invisible Bond,* I describe some of the lies ingrained in me about sex, men and God because of past sex experiences. Ephesians 5:11 and 13-14 says, "Have nothing to do with the fruitless deeds of darkness, but rather expose them...everything exposed to the light becomes visible, for it is light that makes everything visible."

- What is one truth that God has made visible for you regarding your sexual past?

- Read 2 Corinthians 7:1. Lies from our sexual experiences contaminates our bodies, minds and spirits. How have the lies you've believed contaminated your body? Mind? Spirit?

Don't be concerned if you don't know yet. Keep asking God to continue His work of purifying you of the lies that are controlling your body, mind and spirit. In Isaiah 61:1 God promises to bind up our broken hearts, set us free from our captivity and release us from our darkness. His will is to set us free. And what will set us free?

Truth.

In John 8:32 Jesus said, "Then you will know the truth and the truth will set you free." Are you tired of living in darkness? Are you sick of the lies that control you? Want to be free? Then ask God to expose the lies that are contaminating you and replace them with His truth.

Get ready to see everything in a new light—God's healing light of truth.

Think About It…

- What's the most significant truth you've learned this week? Write out the verse (if applicable) that God used to speak to you.

- What is God asking you to do with this new truth?

- Write out your response (prayer) to God here:

CHAPTER SEVEN

Godly Anger

Day One: Our Anger

Are you afraid of anger? Bear with me—it may seem like a silly question on the surface, but take a moment to think about it. Does being angry scare you? What about having others angry at you? For most of my life anger terrified me. I spent a great deal of energy ensuring that others never got angry with me, and an equal amount stuffing or denying my own anger. It was exhausting. You see if someone was angry at me it meant that I was bad, and if I got angry it meant that I was, you know, *bad*—even worse, 'un-Christian'.

Anger for me was a sign that I was unspiritual, back-slidden—a hopeless sinner. I would ask God to forgive me for my anger and try very hard to control it. When I failed again and again, my hopelessness increased. For some reason it seemed like God was rejecting me. I believed He had ceased to answer my prayers. All of that confirmed that I must be bad— even more, that God was angry at me.

But guess what? I had it all wrong. Anger is simply an emotion—one that God created in us. How could God be upset with us for something He gave us? Then I learned from one of my studies that God Himself got angry! Even Jesus expressed anger, but all without sin.

Now I get it. The emotion of anger isn't the problem--it's what we do with the anger that's sin. So how angry are you? Before I went through my own healing I would have said that I wasn't angry at all. But as I've learned, anger isn't just measured by outbursts, but also in other, less obvious ways.

Anger internalized over years can display itself in depression, anxiety, feelings of lowered self-worth, resentment, bitterness, jealousy, and the list goes on. Why don't you take the Anger Questionnaire and see for yourself.

Anger Questionnaire

The following questionnaire will help you determine if anger is a part of your daily life. Many of us suppress anger. Yet the anger still exists and manifests itself in different ways. Use this questionnaire to identify ways you may suppress and/or express anger. Take a few moments to read through the statements below. Pause and re-read them if necessary. Place a check mark by those that apply to our life. Double or triple check mark them if you feel led to do so[21].

_____I get upset with people pressuring me to make a decision

_____It really bothers me when I am not in charge or able to control, change or direct situations or circumstances.

_____I feel very angry when it seems as though I have been "used" by a non-caring person.

_____It's my opinion that others will use me to get sex.

_____When pressured to have sex, I become angry (even when it is my husband).

_____If someone tells me the truth, even though it hurts, I can handle it. But when someone lies to me or deceives me, I become extremely angry with them.

_____I am depressed easily when I fail or do something wrong.

_____I nag those closest to me, even though I know better.

_____Once I become hurt or angry, I cannot control my crying or frustration.

_____Aggressive people who are out for their own gain really bug me.

_____Being misunderstood or judged unfairly is something I cannot handle.

_____Stress or feeling overwhelmed is something I cannot handle. Sometimes I explode.

_____When I think of being used or wounded by others in my sexual past I feel hatred towards them.

_____I hate being alone, left out, overlooked, forgotten or left behind.

_____Self-centered people make me angry.

_____If I have someone in my life to whom my voiced opinion does not mean much, I get terribly frustrated with them.

_____The more uncomfortable I become in a situation, the more sarcastic I am. I may even smile and laugh while inside I am far from happy.

_____I can't stand it when people ignore me, won't listen to my opinion or interrupt me when I'm talking.

- How did you do? Look back over your answers. On a scale of 1-10 with 10 being the extreme, how angry are you? Ask God to show you.

I can imagine how you're feeling. Having stuffed that anger down deep for years you thought you were coping rather well—not even aware that it was there. Now it's surfaced and you're angry at everything and everyone—including *me*. Don't be discouraged. Now that the anger has been identified we can do something about it. You can begin to let it go.

Let God have your anger.

The following exercise will help you do that. I call it "Assigning Responsibility." The first time I was presented with this exercise and asked to divide the circle into sections attributing names of those who shared in responsibility for my pain, I sat there blank. It was no one else's fault but mine. Only one name belonged there. Just as I was about to write my own name across the circle in big letters our leader said, "You must put other names in your circle—it cannot just be yours."

"How did she know what I was thinking?" I pondered. Then I realized we were all thinking the same thing. Regardless of the source of our pain—caused by our own choices or someone else's forced upon us, we all assumed responsibility. No wonder we were so angry. Shouldering all that responsibility was more than we could bear. It's the same for you. What pain did you cause yourself? What trauma did others force on you? Either way, you were not alone. Others had a part in your choices, in your circumstances, in your pain.

Whether it was parents who weren't there for you or who hurt you; friends pressuring you; older siblings teaching or modeling similar behavior; or teachers, lovers, our society, or the enemy scheming against you—the circumstances of your past are not your responsibility alone. It's time to acknowledge the truth.

Don't be afraid. Yes this will be painful. It will stir up anger and hurt. Memories of betrayal by others will resurface. You'll get angry. Don't be afraid of your anger. The anger isn't bad. It's a God-given emotion. It can protect us and others when expressed appropriately. This exercise will help you do that.

Assigning Responsibility Exercise

Start by praying. Ask God to show you who shares responsibility for the circumstances of your sexual past. Whether it includes abuse, rape, pornography, abortion, sexual promiscuity, or homosexuality--others contributed to what you've been exposed to. You didn't have sex alone, you didn't perform your own abortion, you never knew pornography existed before someone showed you or you stumbled upon someone's stash. As God brings names to mind, add a new slice to your pie and write them in the sections.

Are you amazed? I was when I did this exercise. For twenty-five years I never allowed anyone to share responsibility with me. Now it seemed I was leaving no one out—including myself. How was it for you? Do you feel a little lighter now? Sharing the responsibility lifts some of our burden. But we've just begun. Acknowledging that you're angry is the beginning. Assigning sources for your anger is the second step in the process. Tomorrow we'll begin the next crucial step in letting go of your anger.

Why don't you finish today by asking God to expose the extent and source of your anger this week? Ask Him to heal your wounded, angry heart and give you peace.

Day Two: Letting God Have Our Anger

Now you need to express your anger in a letter to each person in your circle. You heard me correctly. Every person gets an anger letter. No, you're not going to give them these letters. I repeat—do not give the people in your circle the letters you are about to write. They are between you and God. There is a chance that after your healing is complete God may have you share honestly with someone in your life about how you feel, especially if that person is in your life now—a spouse, parent, or a friend. However, that is not the purpose of this exercise, nor your ultimate goal. Without that pressure, you can be completely open and honest about how you feel regarding each person's participation or non-participation in your circumstances.

As you begin here are some guidelines:

- In Ephesians 4:26, the Bible says to be angry but not to sin. How do we do that? One way is to use "I" statements instead of "you" statements. "I" statements express how you feel about the other's behavior. "You" statements are critical and judgmental. Let me illustrate: "You were a lousy drunk." versus, "I felt afraid and unloved when you drank."

- Have some quiet, uninterrupted time. Take some time to pray and ask God to guide you. Start with "Dear_____."

- There's no limit to the length of your letter. Some may be very short, others quite long. Just keep writing until you have said all you need to.

- Don't rush. If you want to be done with the anger towards that person you need to take the time to express all you need to say. If not you may find yourself having to go back and rewrite this letter.

- Keep your letters in a safe place where no one can find them.

As you work through the chapter on anger this week, and as you write your letters, I pray that God will release you from any bitter roots of anger that have taken up residence in you. In its place I pray that God will fill you with His peace, love, joy and forgiveness. We're going to talk about forgiveness another week.

This is a valuable exercise that you can use again and again. It's not just restricted to anger from your sexual past. It will work for anger today, anger tomorrow--whatever the reason.

May God bless you as you trust Him to work out His healing in your life using this step. Use the rest of today to write your anger letters. You will continue to write your letters this week as you work through the remainder of this week's lesson. If you're doing this study with others, you'll be reading some of your letters to your group this week. Writing out our feelings is crucial in order to acknowledge how other others have hurt us, but reading them aloud allows the emotion to be expressed. Having others validate our pain and anger is an important part of the healing process. If you're doing the study on your own, be sure to read them to your support person this week.

Day Three: God's Anger

Acknowledging and addressing my anger was a big part of my healing--which is why I want you to experience it too. What helped me most in discovering my anger was learning the truth about God's and Jesus' anger. I'd been afraid of coming to God because I assumed He was angry at me because of my sin. Yes, God is angered by sin. But even more than the sin, God is angry for how the sin hardens our hearts and turns us away from Him. But the moment we come to God with a humble, repentant heart, God's response is never anger, but compassion, forgiveness and grace. Let's look at some verses to learn more about God's anger.

Read the following verses. How is God's anger described?

Deuteronomy 29:28

2 Kings 22:13

Psalm 90:11

- Are you afraid of God's anger? Why or why not?

- What causes God to get angry?

Deuteronomy 9:7

1 Kings 11:9-10

Proverbs 6:16-19

- Has God ever had cause to be angry with you? For what?

- How does God express His anger in these verses?

Psalm 30:5

Psalm 78:38-39

Psalm 86:15

Psalm 103:8-10

- How is God's anger different from your anger?

- What can save us from God's anger?

Psalm 130:3-4

Romans 5:8-11

1 Thessalonians 1:10

1 John 1:9

It's wonderfully comforting to know the source of God's anger, the extent of His anger and how He saves us from His anger. A hardened, rebellious heart angers God the most. Why does this cause God anger? Because He loves us so much. When we reject Him, harden our hearts towards Him, I believe God is not only angry, but hurt. Think about yourself. What angers and hurts you more—rejection by someone you love or by a stranger, or enemy? Now imagine how hurt God is by our rejection.

He created us, loves us unconditionally, died for us, pours out blessings and good gifts on us every day, and has promised us eternal life with Him. All of God's actions and thoughts are centered on us…we are always on His mind. And how do we respond to all this love and goodness? Often we forget about Him, reject Him, harden our hearts toward Him, go our own way. And yet, even in His hurt, He doesn't hold anything against us, but keeps pouring out His love on us.

Even more reassuring is that God's anger is slow, abounding in love, full of compassion and grace. I'd much rather be at the mercy of God's wrath than my own—even on my good days. But that's not all. God lovingly provides a way out from under His wrath. So with a love that defies explanation or understanding, God's anger melts into forgiveness. God cannot resist a repentant heart.

- Read Psalm 51. What will God not despise or reject?

- What's the condition of your heart? Mark it on the line below.

Hardened/Rebellious   Broken/Repentant

$\longleftarrow$ ——————————————————————— $\longrightarrow$

Day Four: Jesus' Anger

God getting angry may not be a surprise to you. Like me, you may have grown up trying to avoid God's anger. You were never quite sure when He was angry at you, but you knew He was capable of it.

But not Jesus. Jesus was all about loving your enemies, turning the other cheek. He never got angry, right? Wrong. Jesus was God in the flesh. And He experienced all the same emotions we do—anger, sadness, joy. With one exception—He was sinless. That means He (as God) could express anger without sin. Let's have a look at what made Jesus angry and how He expressed His anger.

- Read John 2:13-16. What made Jesus angry?

- How did He express His anger?

This passionate display of anger may seem uncharacteristic for Jesus—one we associate with love and forgiveness, until you understand what Jesus was really angry about. He wasn't angry because some animals were being sold in the temple. He was angry that people who came to pray and worship Him were being taken advantage of. Knowing that animals would be needed for sacrifices, merchants sold them at unreasonable prices. Money changers used the opportunity to exploit those who needed to exchange goods for money. People in need, coming to pray and worship, were being preyed upon by the greedy. Those who had much were profiting from those who had very little. Jesus had had enough. As you will see, Jesus is fiercely protective of those who are being victimized, abused, or mistreated. He responds in anger to those taking advantage of others—especially the defenseless, the helpless, the weak, the poor, the alien.

- Mark 3:1-6. What made Jesus angry?

- Read Luke 11:37-52. Why is Jesus angry with the Pharisees?

- Read Luke 17:1-2. Who is Jesus angry at here? Why?

- According to these verses describe in your own words what makes Jesus angry?

- Does Jesus ever sin when He expresses His anger?

What I discovered as I studied these verses is that the motivation for Jesus' anger is other people. He is angry at what is happening to others. This is righteous anger. Usually my anger is because of what someone has done to me. My sense of self-righteousness is ignited and my anger explodes. That is not the kind of anger Jesus expressed. When people mistreated Him, He asked God to forgive them. When others were mistreated, Jesus got angry, defended them, protected them and rescued them.

We are capable of righteous anger too. We can step in to defend someone who is being mistreated, abused or deceived. I remember as an elementary student there was a boy in my class everyone picked on. It made me so angry. He didn't do anything to deserve such abuse. His crime was being different—quiet, less sociable. I was the only one who was nice to him, and I stood up for him to the others in class. I'm not saying this to boast. After all, I was only six and I didn't always do it perfectly. I just want to share with you how anger and the desire to defend someone is an example of how we can express righteous anger on behalf of others.

Another way I put my anger to good use is in volunteering at Alternatives Pregnancy Center, a non-profit crisis pregnancy center. As the Director of Sexual Health Education, I've been privileged to speak truth into young peoples' lives about sex, love and relationships to counteract the lies they're hearing from others. My passion comes from a desire to protect young people from becoming further victims of the sexual revolution as I was. Motivated by God's love, I want to make sure they hear the truth before they're hurt.

- How is your anger different from Jesus' anger?

- What warning does God give us in Ephesians 4:26-27 about our anger?

- How do you sin when you express your anger? What do you do and say when you're angry?

- Who is often the recipient of your anger?

- How has your anger hurt others in your life?

- What does God mean by not letting the sun go down on our anger? Why does He give this warning?

- How would you like to be more like Jesus in the area of expressing anger?

Day Five: Bitter Root

"In your anger do not sin. Do not let the sun go down while you are angry, and do not give the devil a foothold" (Ephesians 4:26-27).

Anger is progressive. Did you know that? That's why God warns us not to let the sun go down on our anger. God knows us well. When we allow anger to simmer longer than a day, there is potential for resentment to set in. As we dwell on resentment, it leads to bitterness. Bitterness can lead to rage. Had a fit of rage recently? Very possibly it stemmed from some overly simmered anger.

- Read Ephesians 4:31. List all the things anger can progress to. Which ones do you suffer from?

The longer we dwell on our anger, the greater hold it has on us. The deeper its roots go—roots of bitterness. How can you tell if your anger toward someone has progressed to a bitter root? By how easily you're angered by small, insignificant things. As I allowed God to examine my anger, He revealed how it had progressed to bitterness towards my husband. I noticed that I was easily angered over the smallest things--some days he just had to walk into the room and I'd be get angry. Can you relate?

- Pray and ask God to reveal any bitter roots you have growing. Who do you have a bitter root towards?

- Instead of anger, what does God want us to be rooted in according to Ephesians 3:17?

- Read Ephesians 3:18-19. What's the result of being rooted in love?

- According to the following verses, if you're rooted in love how will you respond to someone who has hurt you or been angry with you?

Romans 12:17-21

Ephesians 4:32

Colossians 3:12-14

When we've been hurt, used, or wounded by others in our past, we often respond in anger. That causes others to respond in anger back to us. Then feeling misunderstood and mistreated, we become angrier. Sound familiar?

When we experience healing for the hurts of our past, there is no longer a need to protect ourselves. Instead we respond differently because we're now able to perceive the situation from the other person's perspective. Let me illustrate. One evening my husband came home in a nasty mood. Regardless of what I said, his rebuttal was offensive and rude. I felt his disdain was unjustified. But instead of lashing back (my initial reaction), I asked God to help me see what was at the root of my husband's behavior.

The result was nothing short of miraculous. My perspective changed. Rather than feeling sorry for myself, I felt sympathy for my husband. Instead of giving him a piece of my mind, I asked for a piece of his with questions like: "Have I said or done anything to upset you? Is there something bothering you that I can help you with?" And guess what? He *was* upset about something—totally unrelated to me. Although unwarranted, he was taking out his frustration on me—in anger.

With me staying calm, his anger dissolved. Talking it out together dismantled the wall between us. This was completely different from what it could have been, or what it usually became—a heated, hurtful exchange of angry words, exacting emotional damage to each other. What a wise God we have when He advises us in Proverbs 15:1, "A gentle answer turns away wrath, but a harsh word stirs up anger."

- How have you seen the above verse work in your own life?

Expressing love and forgiveness when we've been hurt or mistreated isn't easy. In fact, it's impossible without the supernatural love of God giving us the strength. Did you get that? Responding in anger is the *easy* way out. That's why it's natural for us. Offering love and forgiveness takes strength. It's harder to say "I'm sorry" first, especially when we've been wronged.

Why would we say sorry if we're the ones being mistreated—you may ask? Because most likely if someone has lashed out at you it came from a place of hurt as well. Your apology may be for the unintended hurt you've caused them.

God gave me a great example of this. Recently I was expressing my opinion on a hotly debated topic at a board meeting. A senior member of the board mistook my comments as an indication of my lack of support for him personally. In his attempt to express his feelings he reacted unkindly towards me. I was humiliated, hurt and angry.

As I left that evening I could barely see ahead of me for the angry tears welling up in my eyes. Instead of responding like I usually do—nursing my wounds, I asked God to show me His perspective on the situation. Guess what came to mind immediately? Not my pain, not how I had been mistreated. Instead I saw how my comments had caused my fellow board member pain. Even though there was no malicious intent on my part, I could see how he may have perceived it as such. With this revelation, my anger melted away. In its place came a sorrow for how my words had wounded him. That is Godly sorrow—being sorry for how our actions or words hurt others.

When I got home I emailed him an apology for how my words had hurt him, and an affirmation of my support for him. Honestly, this was new for me. In the past I would have nurtured that anger for some time, allowing it to burrow deep roots of resentment. What a sweet victory. I slept peacefully that night—I had not let the sun go down on my anger. But even more than a good night's sleep, I denied the enemy a foothold in my heart and prevented a bitter root taking up residence.

No surprise—God knows what He's talking about.

Think About It...

- What's the most significant truth you've learned this week? Write out the verse (if applicable) that God used to speak to you.

- What is God asking you to do with this new truth?

- Write out your response (prayer) to God here:

CHAPTER EIGHT

Grieving Your Loss

Day One: The Bible on Grief

We normally associate grief with death. Healthy grieving after the loss of someone close to us is essential. Without it we stay in the pain of our loss, and often end up developing unhealthy ways to deal with our sorrow. According to psychologists, the stages of grief are denial, anger, bargaining, depression and finally acceptance.

The same can happen with the losses associated with our sexual pasts. You may not be aware of it, but you've been grieving. Along with the wounds of sex comes a sense of loss. What have you lost because of your sexual past? Your innocence, youth, ability to trust, love, enjoy life? Your dreams, expectations, health, relationships? What about your self-worth, virginity, chance at a lifetime marriage? And the worst loss of all—never being able to go back and do it all over again. No possibility of a second chance.

Whatever it is, God wants to restore all that you've lost. He wants to resurrect all that's been taken from you—all that's been destroyed or stolen. Just like we can't resurrect a loved one who's passed away, physically there are things we've lost that can't be replaced on this side of heaven. But there is much that God can restore when we say yes to Him and allow Him access to our lives.

- How has the enemy used sex to destroy you?

- Do you believe Jesus can restore life to you in these areas? Why or why not?

- Remember Joel 2:25? Read it again and write out the verse here.

- What does God say He's going to do?

Regardless of the years we've lost to the devastation of our sexual pasts, God wants to restore all that's been lost—and restore it as if it was never taken.

- Do you believe God *can* do this for you? Why or why not?

- Do you believe He *will*?

Trusting God to do what He says is exactly how He wants your heart to respond. Regardless of how many "years" it's been, God can restore them all--but you need to surrender your past to Him.

If you haven't already, what's keeping you from surrendering your past to God?

Day Two: Regret

Have you ever lost something valuable? What did you do to find it? I imagine, like me, its search became your first priority. In addition to expending physical and mental energy to find it, your emotions were like a rollercoaster. There was desperation to find it, regret at having lost it and yet hope that it would be found.

Our messy sexual pasts ignite all the same emotions: desperation, loss and regret. The only thing missing is hope. You see, hope is unknown to us until we can move beyond denial and acknowledge our pain—to ourselves and to God. That's what catapults us out of the darkness and into God's light. Now we have hope. Now we can examine all the lies and the emotions from God's perspective and replace them with His truth.

Understanding why we feel a sense of loss and regret is an essential part of the journey. We feel regret because we sense the loss. So what have we lost? What gives us a hopeless sense of regret? To answer that question, God drew my attention to two verses.

- Read 1 Corinthians 6:18, then fill in the blanks: "Flee from _____ _____. All other sins a man (or woman) commits are _____ his (her) body, but he (she) who sins _____ sins against his (her)_____ body."

  - Who do we sin against when we are sexually immoral?

  - How is that different from other sins?

  - 1 Thessalonians 4:3-6 says, "It is God's will that you should be sanctified: that you should avoid sexual immorality, that each of you should learn to control his own body in a way that is holy and honorable, not in passionate lust like the heathen, who do not know God, *and that in this matter no one should wrong his brother (or sister) or take advantage of him (her)."* What is God's will for us?

  - What does "in this matter" refer to?

  - How is our brother (or sister) wronged or taken advantage of when we engage in sexual immorality with them?

  - How are we wronged?

Even though I'd read those verses many times, God opened my eyes to see something I hadn't realized before. When God says we sin against ourselves, He means that *everything sexually wrong that we've done to the other person, we've also done to ourselves.* The Thessalonians passage says that when we use someone sexually outside marriage, we are wronging them and taking advantage of them. In some translations, the word for taking advantage is translated "defraud". To defraud is to rob someone of something.

- What do we rob others of when we commit sexual sins?

Ultimately, they are robbed of a special God-given gift that is meant for one person—their future spouse. But additionally, they are robbed of the true love and intimacy that goes along with that gift in marriage. They're robbed of intimacy with God, of human dignity, of trust and the ability to bond with one person for life. They're robbed of saving sexual desire and arousal for their future spouse. They're robbed of an unattached and pure mind, body, soul, and spirit. And if we go a step further, we realize that the person's future spouse is robbed of all of these treasures as well.

Why does sexual sin hurt us so much? Because the very first time we engage in sex outside God's plan—in that precise moment our eyes are opened. Sex is no longer a curious mystery or a desire yet to be satisfied. In an instant our hearts know that this is indeed something special, something holy, and something divine.

And something lost.

We've taken a valuable treasure from the other person. *And we've also robbed ourselves.* We now know that we've cheated ourselves of something that can never be replaced, and the remorse, the regret, the pain settle deep into our souls.

- What do you regret about your sexual past?

- What part of your regret is a result of your own sin?

- What part of your regret is a result of someone else's sin?

- What does God want to do with your regret? (2 Corinthians 7:10)

- What will leave no regret?

We're going to talk more about the difference between godly sorrow and worldly sorrow during the forgiveness chapter. In the meantime ask God to give you His perspective on your regret and what is at its root.

Day Three: Shame

I lived with shame for twenty-five years. Just looking at the word reminds me of its relentless torture. I assumed my feeling of shame meant that God hadn't forgiven me—so I'd ask Him to, again and again. I was wrong. Shame was not evidence that God was unwilling to forgive. He does not withhold His forgiveness from us. When we accept Him as our Savior, His gift of forgiveness encompasses *all* our past, present and future sins.

So what was causing my shame? Why is it that now, after I've brought my sins into His light, the shame is gone? The first recorded account of shame takes us right back to the beginning of creation with Adam and Eve. Let's take a look at their experience.

- Read Genesis 2:15-3:11. Before Adam and Eve eat from the Tree of Good and Evil, what are they wearing? Do they know what shame is?

- What's the first thing that happens when they eat from the tree?

- How do they feel about being naked?

- How is their relationship with God different now?

I'll never forget a life-changing moment when Satan vigorously used shame to condemn me, but God used it to draw me to Him—and God won. I had been given a tremendous honor and responsibility. The Senior Pastor of our church called to see if I would consider serving on the Leadership Team for the church. God confirmed it as I prayed for an answer. So I said yes. In a get-to-know-you game on a Pastor's and Board Member's retreat, I came face to face with a sea of shame.

"Tell us how you met. What did you do on your first date? What did you do on your first five dates?" were the intrusive questions being asked of us as everyone looked on. I wanted to die. I felt exposed as shame stabbed me over and over. I couldn't very well answer—"we had sex by our fifth date." Not the "board member' kind of answer they were looking for. The trauma of that moment has erased my memory of what we did say—but I know we made something up.

The next morning during my quiet time with God, the enemy's taunting of, "If they really knew about your past, they never would have asked you on the board," ran through my mind. I sat before God thinking that He must agree with that statement. But God had a wonderful gift for me that morning. He showed me that He did not see me the way I saw myself. I saw the filth, the ugliness. Miraculously, because of Christ shedding His blood for me, He saw me unblemished, holy, and perfect--not because I was, but because Christ was and now God saw me through Jesus.

This is the verse God gave me: *"How much more then will the blood of Christ who through the eternal Spirit offered himself unblemished to God, cleanse our consciences from acts that lead to death so that we may serve the living God"* (Hebrews 9:14).

Jesus took all our sin *on Himself*—all our ugliness and filth was on Him at His death—not on us. Because of what Jesus did, when we receive His gift of forgiveness, God doesn't see our sin anymore—He sees Jesus, unblemished, holy, righteous.

Is that too awesome for you to grasp? It was for me that day. I sat weeping with gratitude and amazement at such a miracle of grace. It changed me. When I realized that God didn't see me as a filthy sinner, I had the courage to bring my ugliness into the open—into His healing light.

God very much wants to remove your shame. Read these verses and marvel at how much God loves you. What does God want to do for you according to these verses?

Isaiah 54:4-8

Isaiah 61:1-3, 7

Ezekiel 16:8-14

Joel 2:25-26

Ephesians 5:25-27

Day Four: Grief

I have an aversion to pain. I avoid it at all costs. When I do experience it, I don't like it. And when I'm in pain, I insist others suffer with me—if not in reality, than experientially through my groaning and moment by moment descriptions of each painful detail. It's pathetic, I admit. Thankfully my husband loves me enough to endure my shameless appeal for sympathy with grace.

For most of us the same thing applies to emotional pain. We avoid it too.

First we do our best to deny it, and when we can't any longer we learn to cope using whatever appeals to us and is readily available. (By now God has already shown you your particular pain-relieving drug of choice, and you're working on replacing that with something healthy). But then something interesting happens. Our coping strategy starts causing us pain. It's like a drug—the more we take it, the more we want it. However, the more we take it, the less it works at making us feel better—so the more of it we *need*.

Our coping mechanism starts causing us pain when it begins to interfere with our lives, relationships and work. If we're drinking when we should be making dinner for our family--they get angry at us. If we avoid physical and emotional intimacy with our spouse by staying up reading or watching TV instead of going to bed—our marriage suffers. That's painful. But even more painful is the realization that our unhealthy coping strategy now has a hold on us and won't let go. This new pain often masks the original culprit of our circumstances—the one that will be necessary to discover and address.

Our coping mechanisms are an example of bad pain. In contrast, good pain is being willing to submit to the grieving process. The Bible talks about grief. Some of God's most trusted, faithful servants experienced grief, sadness, depression and anxiety. We're in good company. In fact, God talks about the healing quality of grief. Let's take a look.

126

- Read Ecclesiastes 7:3. What does it mean 'sorrow is better than laughter'? How will a heart be made better with sorrow?

- Read Hebrews 5:8-9. Who is this verse talking about? What did He learn through suffering?

Stop and think about this for a moment. Jesus—the perfect son of God, sinless and holy, learned obedience through suffering. Go back and read verse seven of this passage. Jesus grieved as He prepared to take our sins to the cross. He grieved for us. He grieved over the sin that separated us from God. Isaiah 53 says, "He was a man acquainted with sorrows and grief."

Jesus is our example. He embraced suffering and grief and through it learned obedience—not that He was disobedient, but He was being called to obedience unlike ever before, just like you and me. How is it that we are so desperate to avoid the very thing that Jesus will use in our lives to teach us obedience and bring us healing? That's right—we hate pain. Yet our pain-avoidance strategies are actually more painful than what God will use for our healing. When will we absorb the truth that God offers us more grace than we offer ourselves?

Grief has an amazing benefit. It breaks our hearts. Now that may not sound so appealing. But believe me when I say that unless our hearts are broken, there's nothing to heal. In contrast, a hardened heart sees no need for healing. Blinded by self-reliance, self-protection and self-rationalization, the eyes of a hardened heart turn inward, not upward. Isaiah 61:1 says that God has come to bind up our broken hearts. My prayer for you is that God will break your heart so He can also bind it up.

- How does God feel about your broken heart?

Isaiah 57:15

Isaiah 66:2

- What will He do for your broken heart?

Psalm 51:12

Matthew 11:28-30

- What does God promise for those in mourning?

Psalm 30:11-12

Isaiah 40:1-2

Isaiah 51:3

Isaiah 54:4-8

Isaiah 61:1-3, 7

To repeat what I said on day one, you've been grieving. You may not be aware of it because you've done your best to ignore it. Unfortunately *your* grieving process has been adding to your pain and the pain of those you love. Be willing to embrace God's grieving process. Not only is it grief that will bring health and healing to every part of your being, but once through it you will be done with that pain, that sin—for good.

Day Five: Acceptance

Acceptance is the sweet reward for godly grieving. The tears have been shed. The ache in our heart has subsided. Anxiety is replaced with peace. Sorrow ushers in joy. There is well-earned rest after the hard work is done. Suffering has set us free.

To compare David's emotional and physical condition during his grieving to his experience of freedom read Psalm 30:1-12, and Psalm 38:1-18.

Which David do you relate to more? Is it the one whose back is filled with searing pain, or the one who's dancing and singing for joy? Don't worry if you're still in the suffering part of your grieving. If that's where God wants you to stay, He has a good reason. There's something more He wants you to see--or pain yet to be exposed. Trust Him. He knows you. He loves you. He wants your very best. Let Him have His way with you. If you rush past God, you will need to revisit it again someday. I urge you to avoid more pain—make someday, today.

God uses some wonderful pictures in His word to describe freedom and healing. Some make me smile, some give me strength, but they all describe a soul set free. Read the following passages and answer the questions.

- Psalm 103:1-5. How does God describe someone who is free? (verse 5)

- Isaiah 61:3(b). How does God describe someone who is free?

- Malachi 4:2. How does God describe freedom here? Which one are you—a leaping calf who's been set free or a sauntering cow still burdened by your sin? Or somewhere in-between?

- Read Leviticus 26:13. What yoke does God promise to break?

- Read Job 36:16. How does God describe freedom here? How does a spacious place compare to a restricted place? Which one describes your life?

- Which of the above verses is your favorite? Why?

Where are you right now in the grieving process? Stalled in anger? Struggling with depression? Or does the healing touch of acceptance have you leaping and soaring? Don't despair if you haven't reached acceptance yet. Just keep listening to God's voice. He will direct your path—every move, every step, and even the timing of when you reach your final destination. It's not a race—there is no deadline. It's walking with God, one 'yes' at a time. Doing it His way, in His time, means nothing is wasted. There'll be no "do-over's" because you'll do it right the first time.

Think About It...

- What's the most significant truth you've learned this week? Write out the verse (if applicable) that God used to speak to you.

- What is God asking you to do with this new truth?

- Write out your response (prayer) to God here:

CHAPTER NINE

Forgiveness

Day One: The Passion of Christ

Raised in church since birth, I know all about forgiveness. I can tell you what it means, I can tell you how to get it, and I can even share stories of experiencing it in my life. But when I needed it the most, it eluded me. I'd forgotten the most important thing about forgiveness—that it's free. We can't earn it, we can't buy it, we can't even bargain for it. Most importantly, we don't deserve it--which is why it's a free gift, graciously given by the One whose suffering and death made it possible—Jesus. Jesus is passionate about offering us forgiveness. He gave His life for it. He gave His life so we could have it—free.

Webster's dictionary defines forgiveness as a pardon. To pardon someone means to excuse their offense without enacting a penalty. In other words—cancel their debt. That's exactly what happened when Jesus died on the cross for us. He paid the penalty of our sin *for* us, allowing God to cancel our debt to Him. This is so big. God has canceled the debt of all the sin we've ever done, are doing right now and will do in the future. Incredible, but true.

I know I said forgiveness was free—but there is one thing we need to do. It sounds easy, but doing it can be a challenge. *We need to receive it.* We need to accept what Jesus did for us on the cross, and believe in His power to forgive our sins. Have you ever tried to give someone a gift they won't accept? How did that make you feel? What happened to the gift? Their refusal negated the value of the gift in their life, just as it will in ours when we refuse to accept God's gifts for us.

There was a woman in our neighborhood with five small children. Because of a medical emergency, she needed help during the day caring for her young children while she left for an extended time. A group of women I belonged to called Moms In Touch (an international organization with local groups who pray weekly for their children and schools) offered this woman a gift. We put together a schedule to come and care for her children, clean, do laundry and make meals for as long as she needed us. It was an offer no one could refuse. But *she* did. Her reason? There were many. Primarily, she didn't want to be obligated to us.

She was convinced our gift had a price tag. That eventually she'd have to "pay" us back. Amazing. The concept of a "gift" was lost to her. She's not alone. Sadly, many will be left outside the gates of heaven because they tried to earn the gift of salvation rather than receive it. Why? The main reason is pride. If I can earn it, then I deserve it and that validates me. It makes me "good enough."

It took some convincing on our part, but we finally assured her that our gift was free— free from obligation, free from any reciprocation on her part. With hesitation, she finally accepted our gift. Even if this woman had refused our gift, its value would be unchanged-- but she would have been denied the value of the gift benefiting her and her children's lives.

Many of us have a hard time accepting God's gift of forgiveness. We think if we can earn or buy it, then it has more value, it becomes real. But trying to earn forgiveness negates its value as a gift. And when we spurn a gift, we also reject the One who offers it, and minimize how He suffered and died on our behalf in order to offer it. And so we ask for forgiveness over and over, but, because we can't receive it, the power of this gift to change our lives is lost to us.

- Which one is harder for you? To ask for forgiveness or to accept it?

- What about your sexual past or present do you need to ask forgiveness for?

- When we ask for forgiveness, what does God say He will do with our sins? Read the following verses to answer.

Psalm 51:1-19

Psalm 103:10-12

Isaiah 38:17

Isaiah 43:25

Isaiah 44:22

Jeremiah 31:34

Micah 7:18-19

1 John 1:9

God is passionate about forgiving *you*. He wants to wash you, clean and restore you to Him. In essence what God is saying in the above verses is that He will put your sins out of His sight, out of His reach, out of His mind and out of existence completely. This is the gift of forgiveness from a Holy, loving God. For us—it's free. For God—it cost Him His only Son. For Jesus—He gave His life. But even more, He gave up heaven.

- Read Philippians 2:5-8. Long before Jesus gives up His life on the cross, He gives up other things. List what they are.

I've always focused on Jesus' suffering and death, but what amazed me about this passage is that long before Jesus died on the cross He gave up so much more: His throne in heaven. He went from being served and worshiped to being rejected and scorned. Then, choosing to clothe Himself in flesh and humility, He came as *our* servant. He walked in our shoes, experienced our struggles, cried our tears. Being God, He could have chosen another way to offer us forgiveness. Something more majestic—more royal. More God-like. He could have insisted we come to Him. Instead *He* chose to bend down to *us*—become like us, serve us, suffer with and for us by giving His life. Sounds like an offer no one can refuse.

I can't say no to that—can you?

Day Two: The Root of Sin

It may surprise and relieve you to know that God doesn't have a hierarchy of sin. It may be how we think, but remember God's thoughts are higher than our thoughts. What seems right or fair to us is often opposite to what God judges as right or fair. God says sin is sin. One sin is not greater or less than the other because it all has the same root. I discovered this as I progressed through my healing. As I began to ask God to forgive the "big" things in my life, like the abortion and promiscuous sex, I discovered that He was concerned about something far greater—what caused me to sin.

What was at the root of my sin? Why was it so easy for me to sin to this extent, especially as a Christian? I have to admit this had been a nagging thought on my mind. If I could stoop so low then what would keep me from a repeat or even worse fall now or in the future?

Read my answer in this excerpt from *The Invisible Bond*.[22]

I focused on the sin itself, but God wanted me to see what was at the root of my sin. The root, I learned, is a hardened heart towards God. As I studied great men and women of God in the Bible, I realized that whenever God approached them about the deeds of their sin, He first revealed to them that their actions were just a symptom of what their heart condition was. Once we turn our hearts away from God and stop listening to His voice, we are capable of anything. God doesn't hierarchy sin because there is no limit to the depth of evil a hardened heart can stoop to.

Let's look at some verses to see what God has to say:

- Read Zechariah 7:8-12. What did God ask them to do? Why didn't they do what God asked?

- Read Psalm 95:7-10, Hebrews 3:7, 15-16, 4:7. What led the hearts of Israel astray?

- Read Ephesians 4:18-19. What can happen when we harden our hearts towards God?

- Read Jeremiah 2:13. God is describing two sins that His people have committed. Describe them in your own words.

Let's talk about a hardened heart for a moment. Like me, maybe you've been focusing on the outward things as the source of your problem: what you've done, the things that have been done to you, or your current sexual or relationship struggles. "This is what needs fixing," you may be thinking. Instead God is saying, "Let's look at the condition of your heart. That is what needs to change."

When the condition of our heart is in line with God, our actions fall into place. Many things can cause our hearts to harden. When we are hurt, misused, abandoned or betrayed, our natural instinct is to protect ourselves. In the process, our hearts harden. After sexual trauma, a wounded heart can harden in self-preservation. Subconsciously a hardened heart punishes itself for being vulnerable to hurt; or we punish others for how they've hurt us. We may even punish God, because He couldn't be trusted to protect us from being hurt in the first place. A hardened heart says, "I'm on my own, I'll take care of myself." This is exactly what happens in Jeremiah 2:13. A hardened heart forsakes God and goes his (her) own way.

- What past wound has caused you to mistrust God? Or caused your heart to harden?

- What wrong choices has your hardened heart caused you to make?

- Is God softening your heart? How do you know?

If God is revealing to you that your heart is hardened towards Him, pray Ezekiel 36:26-27. Ask God to remove your heart of stone and give you a heart of flesh. Ask Him to put His Spirit in you to move you to follow Him.

"I will give you a new heart and put a new spirit in you; I will remove from you your heart of stone and give you a heart of flesh. And I will put my Spirit in you and move you to follow my decrees and be careful to keep my laws" (Ezekiel 36:26-27).

Day Three: Godly Sorrow vs. Worldly Sorrow

You just got back from having lunch with a co-worker. During lunch you began talking about your boss. It started out innocent enough but before long, caught up in the conversation, you said some nasty things about your boss. Now it's mid-afternoon and your lunch feels heavy in your stomach. You have this sick feeling that you said too much at lunch. What are you really feeling--guilty or sorry? They may sound like the same thing, but feeling guilty and feeling sorry are two very different responses.

When we become Christians God places His Holy Spirit inside us as a Counselor. He does many things for us. He is the Spirit of Truth and guides us to all truth, He teaches us all things, He helps us pray, He gives us power to do God's will and deny our selfish desires, and He convicts us when we disobey God. That sick feeling you have is not indigestion—it's the Holy Spirit convicting you that your words did not glorify God. Once convicted, we can respond in one of two ways. We can feel guilty or we can feel sorry.

One is a worldly response, the Bible says, and one is godly.

- Read 2 Corinthians 7:10. Write it out here.

- Godly sorrow produces three things. What are they?

- What does worldly sorrow lead to?

What's the difference? Let's go back to our story. If the conviction of the Holy Spirit causes you to react with guilt or worldly sorrow, who are you thinking about? You! Guilt causes us to focus on ourselves and the consequences of what we've done. What if the boss finds out what you said about him? What will happen? Maybe you'll lose your job, or that promotion you were hoping for, or your reputation. After all, you're a Christian. What will people think of you? Can you relate? Have you felt this way when you've been convicted about something you've said or done?

Guilt or worldly sorrow is all about me and how my sin is going to affect me. Paul says that worldly sorrow "brings death." What does he mean by this? He's not only talking about physical death, but spiritual death. When we're motivated by worldly sorry, instead of leading to repentance or change, we move further away from God.

In contrast, godly sorrow makes us sorry—not for us but for the person we've hurt. In our example, if the conviction of the Holy Spirit had made you feel godly sorrow, you would have immediately felt regret for how your words would hurt your boss—not you. This is what God cares about—does our sorrow focus on us or on the one we've hurt? If our focus is on the one we've hurt, then Paul says our sorrow brings repentance. When we see how much we've hurt someone, we'll no longer have a desire for this behavior. We'll turn away from the negative behavior to something positive, leading to change that will leave no regret.

The Scripture gives us a great example of each type of sorrow. Judas, who betrayed Jesus, was convicted, but his sorrow caused him to take his own life. This is worldly sorrow. In contrast, when Peter denied Christ three times before His death, he was also convicted. His response was godly sorrow. He was broken-hearted for what he had done to Christ. His sorrow brought him closer to God, which led to repentance and no regret.

How will you know which one you've experienced? The answer is in the regret. If you keep asking God to forgive you for the same thing over and over but never find relief, then probably your sorrow is worldly. God will continue to convict you until you see it from His perspective. Read the following excerpt from *The Invisible Bond*[23] to see how God used this truth in my life.

I realized that up until now my sorrow had been worldly. How did I know? Because if godly sorrow leaves no regret then worldly sorrow must. Though I'd asked God to forgive me many times, I still felt regret. When I experienced true godly sorrow, my shame and regret were gone.

Drs. Henry Cloud and John Townsend define the difference between godly and worldly sorrow in How People Grow. "Worldly sorrow can keep us from feeling forgiven. [It] is not based in love, but on oneself and one's own badness. On the other hand, godly sorrow focuses on the offended party. The Bible says we should not feel guilty, but we should feel sorry. There is a big difference. Godly sorrow ends up in repentance. When we realize we are hurting someone we love, we change. But guilt, (or worldly sorrow) actually causes sin to increase. It only makes people rebel more."[1]

God demonstrated this for me while praying to break sexual bonds. I made a list of everyone that I had been sexually promiscuous with and starting at the top asked God to break the bonds (more on this later).

Although none of my experiences could be considered sexual abuse, I felt as much a victim with most of them as I did an initiator—many of the men had exerted subtle pressure in this area.

As I prayed, my mind focused more on asking God to forgive them for sinning against me than for me sinning against them. But as I proceeded down my list, something amazing happened. God began to show me what I had committed against these men. I had robbed them just as they had robbed me. He made it clear that I had used these men in my search for love and acceptance instead of going to Him. I didn't really love any of them. I had no intention of marrying them, yet I was willing to use them to fulfill my need. My prayer changed from what they had done to me, to what I had done to them.

I experienced true repentance. For the first time I had no regret. Godly sorrow was the one thing that finally broke the hold my past had on me.

For the first time since my early sexual experiences I didn't feel sorry for me. Instead I felt sorry for the men I had used, and I felt sorry for God. I imagined how much I had hurt Him by ignoring Him in my life.

- Think about your sexual past. Have you had more worldly sorrow or godly sorrow for what's happened?

- Do you see things differently now? How so?

Day Four: Accepting God's Forgiveness

Forgiveness is a gift from God. Like salvation, it's a gift we must accept if we want to experience its benefit in our lives. When we ask God to forgive us but then fail to believe and accept His forgiveness, we leave ourselves vulnerable to Satan's attack of shame. The shaming voice accuses us of our sin over and over, convincing us that its existence is evidence that God's forgiveness has eluded us. Our sin was too horrible, we are bad, and instead of forgiveness being a gift, we must pay for our sin—we are responsible for our own redemption. It's a lie. Don't waste another second believing it.

Despite what you're tempted to believe, God does not have two sin lists—one He will forgive and one He won't. And God doesn't say He'll only forgive each sin once and only once—there is no limitation on God's forgiveness in either the kind of sin or the number of sins we commit. There's only one thing He asks of us. Confession. To confess means we agree with God about our sin. We look at our sin from His perspective and agree with Him on what we've done. We agree that our sin was against His word, His plan and His will for us.

Look up 1 John 1:9. Fill in the blanks: "If we _____ our sins, He is faithful and just and will _____ us our _____ and will _____ us from _____ unrighteousness."

- According to this verse, what is our part? What is God's part?

- What sin(s) is God asking you to confess? Write out your prayer of confession for each sin God brings to mind here:

Forgiveness has two components. One is grace. Grace is when God blesses us with something we don't deserve. Forgiveness is one of those blessings. Instead of forgiveness we deserve punishment. This is where God's mercy comes in. Mercy is when God doesn't give us what we do deserve for our sins—punishment. Grace and mercy—two miracles of God that we've done nothing to deserve, yet God lavishes them on us with abandon.

I want you to take a moment right now and thank God for His incredible gift of forgiveness—for the sacrifice He made on the cross so you could receive it. Tell Him that you accept His gift of forgiveness. Also tell him that you accept His gift of grace which bestows blessings on you that you do not deserve, and His gift of mercy that holds back the punishment you do deserve. Don't forget to tell Him you love Him. There's nothing He'd rather hear—and He loves to hear *your* voice.

Once we accept God's forgiveness we can reject the shame the enemy tries to cripple us with. This releases us to become all that God has created us to be. Below are some verses describing what God has for those who've been forgiven and set free.

- Isaiah 32:17. What is the fruit of righteousness which comes through God's forgiveness?

- Isaiah 35:5-7. What will God do for the one who has received forgiveness?

- Isaiah 43:18-19. What does God want to do in you?

- Isaiah 61:7. What will God replace your shame with?

Ephesians 5:25-27. Although this starts out as a command for husbands to love their wives, it's compared to how Christ loves us and what He's done for us. What has Christ done for us by His forgiveness? How does He present us to Himself?

Day Five: Forgiving Others

"For if you forgive men when they sin against you, your heavenly Father will also forgive you. But if you do not forgive men their sins, your Father will not forgive your sins" (Matthew 6:14-15).

Godly forgiveness is always moving--never still. Forgiveness, according to God's plan, flows from Him to us and then without hesitation flows from us to others. And that's not all—the outflow needs to be proportionate with the flow in. If you have been forgiven much then your forgiveness towards others must be much as well. Sound difficult—impossible even? I know how you feel. Being forgiven is easy--forgiving others, not so fun. One thing I'm learning is that whatever God does for me is not just for me. The ultimate multi-tasker, God loves to multiply His blessings.

- What has God done in your life during this study? Can you make a list?

Whatever God has done for you, He also wants to do in everyone He's put in your life—your children, spouse, family, co-workers, neighbors, friends and enemies. Has He given you forgiveness? He wants you to give it away to others. Has He healed your broken heart? He wants you to share that with others. Has He shown you the truth where you once believed a lie? He wants you to lead others to the same truth as well. Has He filled you with peace, joy and love? Then He expects you to exude that into the lives of others.

- How is God using you to bless others with what He's done in your life?

- How have you been more forgiving towards others because of God's forgiveness to you?

Forgiveness is not a suggestion, it's a command. It's not even a feeling, but a choice. God doesn't say we need to *feel* forgiveness for others, we must choose to offer it. God takes care of the feelings. Choosing to forgive is a step of faith that God honors. Then the feelings follow. I'm not saying forgiveness is easy. Or that it will happen overnight. Although it may take time for feelings of forgiveness to surface, each time an unforgiving thought arises, make a conscious choice once again to forgive. Then trust God that He will take care of your feelings. Because He will.

God used the parable of the unforgiving servant in Matthew 18:21-35 in a powerful way to reveal my unforgiving heart when I was going through my post abortion Bible Study. Before I share what God showed me I'd like you to prayerfully mediate on this passage. Ask God to speak to you.

- Read Matthew 18: 21-35. How much did the servant owe the King compared to how much his fellow servant owed him?

- How does what you've done against God compare with what others have done against you?

- Who have you put in prison, torturing them until they can pay back all the debt they owe you?

- What do you think Jesus means when He says to forgive someone seventy-seven times?

As I absorbed the magnitude of the servant's unmerciful attitude, the truth of my own unforgiving heart overwhelmed me. *I* was that servant. God had forgiven me *so* much and yet I was holding others prisoner for far less crimes against me. Not only had I thrown them into prison, I was torturing them day after day—making them pay—making them sorry they'd ever messed with me. How was I doing that? By taking my love and affection from them, by withdrawing from them emotionally, by holding them to a higher standard than anyone else—including myself. Then when they couldn't live up to my unrealistic expectations, I'd criticize them, ignore them, belittle them. Even hate them.

The truth set me free. And I set my prisoners free. How? By forgiving them. By realizing that their crime against me was nothing compared to my crime against God. If God could forgive me, I could forgive others. Because I wasn't doing it for them—I was doing it for God.

When Jesus tells the disciples to forgive someone seventy-seven times, He's letting them know that forgiveness has no limit—not with Him, and it shouldn't with us. God gave me an example of this when friends hurt us deeply one summer. I was trying to forgive them, but I'd often revisit the pain causing resentful, unforgiving thoughts to rise again. In the past when this happened, I assumed that I hadn't properly forgiven them the first time and needed to do it again. Or that I wasn't really surrendering this to God. But God showed me that one of the ways to forgive seventy-seven times was to have a continual forgiving spirit to the same person for the same offense. In our case there was one offense, but I had to forgive them over and over, whenever the painful thoughts threatened.

Each time I felt resentment, I chose again to forgive them, trusting God to give me the feelings of forgiveness. I'd say something like, "God I choose to forgive _____ for _____. And now I will trust you to give me feelings of forgiveness for them." It didn't happen right away, but over the weeks I noticed that I was thinking of them less and less, until one day I realized that I no longer harbored resentment towards them. While I was being obedient to God in making the choice to forgive, He'd changed my heart to feel forgiveness.

Back in Chapter Six you began to write some anger letters. It's time to forgive all those who have hurt you, used you, betrayed you, lied to you, or been violent against you. It's also time to forgive those who were too weak to support you, believe in you and stand strong for you.

Believe me, it's time. I want you to take each anger letter and write a forgiveness letter. When you're done, place the forgiveness letter over the anger letter to symbolize that God's forgiveness covers our sin and the sins of others against us. It doesn't mean that you've forgotten what they've done, or that the relationship should be reconciled—some people are just not safe for us. It's a reminder that regardless of what you've done against God, He sees you as forgiven. That's the gift He offers us, and the gift He commands us to offer others.

As you write your forgiveness letters here are some things that forgiveness is not:

- *Forgiving is not forgetting.* Forgiving what someone has done and forgetting are two different things and should not be a test of forgiving. When someone is harmful towards us, we can forgive them but acknowledge that although we've forgiven them they are not safe people for us.

- *Reconciliation need not always follow forgiveness.* If you've been molested by someone as a child—say a parent, or family member, etc., you can forgive them without being reconciled to them. If they have not shown repentance or remorse for what they've done and turned away from their sin, they may not be a safe person for you or your family. You may forgive them but need not feel pressured to have them a part of your life.

- *Forgiveness is not excusing.* Forgiveness does not mean you excuse what someone has done. Acknowledging what has been done and how you've been hurt is important for you and the other person. This allows them to ask your forgiveness and God's forgiveness. Excusing someone usually keeps actions in the dark, while loving confrontation with forgiveness allows it to come into God's light. Everyone—the offender and offended benefits from this.

- *Forgiveness is:* A choice, not a feeling. God commands us to choose to forgive. We can trust Him to make our feelings catch up with our actions.

- *Forgiveness is for your sake.* Forgiving others sets us free from another's hold on us.

- *Forgiveness is agreeing to live with the consequences of another person's sin.* You will live with them anyway, so you can choose to do so in the bondage of bitterness or in the freedom of forgiveness.[24]

- *We follow Jesus' example.* He forgave His crucifiers although they did not ask for His forgiveness.

Think About It...

- What's the most significant truth you've learned this week? Write out the verse (if applicable) that God used to speak to you.

- What is God asking you to do with this new truth?

- Write out your response (prayer) to God here:

CHAPTER TEN

Holy Sex

Day One: Song of Songs Part I

God is not ashamed of sex. In fact, He dedicated an entire book in the Bible to sex, romance and marriage using the relationship between Solomon and his bride. If your "sex senses" have been dulled over the years, get ready for some racy reading. After studying this book I was captivated by God's passion and excitement for marital sex. I know you will be too.

Your assignment this week will seem a little odd, but I hope you've grown to trust me enough to give a wholehearted effort. I guarantee God will honor your sincere attempts even if you feel like you're not getting anything out of it.

The book Song of Songs, or Song of Solomon, is found tucked between Ecclesiastes (following Proverbs) and Isaiah. It's some of the sexiest reading you'll ever encounter. Every day for the next five days during your devotion time, I want you to read the entire book of Song of Songs. Yes, the entire book. It won't take you more than fifteen minutes. Before you read, ask God to show you at least one truth you can meditate on that day. After you're finished, I want you to write down the verse(s) or truth that seems to leap off the page for you or one you think God is speaking to you through, even if you're not sure what it means or how to apply it.

Next I want you to ask God how this truth applies to your past or your present sex life or relationship. Maybe He wants to reveal a truth that is contrary to what you've believed about sex. What lie about sex, yourself, the opposite sex or even God does He want to replace with this truth?

After you've answered these two questions, I'll have some other insights that you can look at that God has shown me. I pray that God's truth through His word will penetrate into the deepest, darkest places of your heart where the enemy has convinced you of his lies. God's truth not only transforms our minds, which affect our attitudes and our actions, but it also sets us free. I pray that you'll experience exhilarating freedom that lasts forever this week.

Before you begin, let me give you some helpful background into this book. Solomon was David's son who became king of Israel after David's death. When God offered to give Solomon whatever he desired, Solomon asked God for wisdom. God was pleased with his request and made him the wisest man to ever live, as well as one of the wealthiest. Solomon wrote three books: Song of Songs, Proverbs and Ecclesiastes. It is believed that Song of Songs was written at the beginning of his life, Proverbs during mid-life and Ecclesiastes at the end. Solomon went on to have 700 wives and 300 concubines.

Acquiring so many wives was not God's will for him, and having so many, especially those from other religions, led to his downfall and ultimate turning away from God. You're not alone if you find Solomon's choice to acquire so many wives distasteful, and puzzling. Why would God use someone who seemed to undervalue marriage as His messenger?

I hear you. But regardless of the messenger God used, the message is still the same, and it's still His message. Thankfully He chooses to use sinful, broken people to speak His truth, and Solomon is one of those He chose to reveal His truth about love, marriage and sex. It's also important to know that Solomon inherited many wives from his father, who also inherited wives from the king before him—which was the custom at that time. Also, wives were acquired for political and other official purposes. In this case, at the beginning of his reign, Solomon was in love with this woman, and chose her to be his queen. Don't let the fact that Solomon went on to acquire more wives deter you from discovering God's truth for you in this book.

- Read the entire book of Song of Songs. What verse or truth stands out for you today?

- How does this new truth impact you today? Is there something about yourself, sex, others or God that He wants you to see differently?

Verse one starts out with the beloved (bride) desiring Solomon to kiss her. "Let him kiss me with the kisses of his mouth." How many of you gave your kisses (virginity) away before you were married, and now that you're married you struggle with not having the same desire today?

- If so, why do you think that is?

- Song of Songs 1:6 (NIV) says, "My own vineyard I have neglected." What do you think "vineyard" means here?

Theologically, vineyard is used to refer to her body. In taking care of her family's vineyard, she neglected to take care of her own body. Her dark appearance, in a culture that values milky-white skin, makes her feel self-conscious and unworthy.

God used this verse to impress upon me that I had neglected my "vineyard" as well. In giving away my virginity carelessly before marriage, I neglected to honor my body and virginity as God wanted me to. Like Solomon's bride, neglecting my body sexually had caused me to feel self-conscious, shameful and unworthy about my sexuality.

- How have you neglected your vineyard or virginity?

- How has that wounded you? Do you feel self-conscious of your body? Your sexuality?

Day Two: Song of Songs Part II

Are you ready for more sexy reading? I can hear some of you saying, "What sexy reading? I didn't get anything out of it." Don't be alarmed if that is you. The first time I read through this book, the only thing that stood out for me was when the beloved talks about neglecting her vineyard. Everything else seemed to be written in a different language. Actually, it is--kind of. I'm relieved my husband doesn't call me a mare, or tell me that my teeth are like a "flock of sheep just shorn."

As we progress through this book, you'll discover that there are some code words that the lover and beloved use to talk sexy to each other. Ask God to open your eyes to see what they are. I assure you, once you start to decipher the code words, you may actually begin to blush as you read.

As you read through the book, remember to ask God to show you one or more verses or truths that are just for you today. Then ask Him how these truths apply to you specifically.

- Read the entire book of Song of Songs. What is a verse or truth that stood out for you?

- How does this new truth impact you? Is there something about yourself, sex, others or God that He wants you to see differently?

- Read Song of Songs 1:9-11, 15. How does the lover see his beloved?

- Read 1:5-6, and 2:1. How does the beloved's description of herself change from chapter one to chapter two? What do you think caused this change?

- How do you see yourself? Like the beloved in chapter one or in chapter two?

- Who have you looked to in determining your worth as a woman?

- Who should you look to?

- What do you think Chapter 2:7 means?

- If you awakened your sexual pathway before marriage, how has that impacted your desire in marriage?

- Read 2:10-13. Are you ready for God to do something new in your present or future marital relationship? What is it you want God to make new for you in this area of sex?

- Read 2:15. What do you think the foxes are?

- What are some of the foxes in your marriage relationship now? Or in the past if you're single again?

- If you've never been married, what foxes did you allow in your past relationships?

- How can you ensure that you avoid these foxes in a future relationship?

Day Three: Song of Songs Part III

Have you noticed that the beloved has sex on her brain? Seriously, she seems to think about sex, talk about sex, and desire sex with Solomon even more than he does. What's up with that? Does her enthusiasm for sex seem a little unrealistic, even *unspiritual* to you? It did to me when I first read it. I certainly didn't share her seemingly over-sexed attitude. But then God reminded me that when I was single I *did* think like her. I loved sex *then*. I was easily aroused *then*. What happened?

God showed me that without realizing it, I associated my desire and enjoyment of sex as a single woman with shame and sin. Because of the negative bonding with sex in my past, I still associated sex with shame as a married woman. This was one of the "foxes" I brought into my marriage. This was what God wanted to protect me from by saving sex for marriage. Now I could see everything clearly. In my pain and shame I had turned my "sex switch" off.

God wanted to turn it on again.

- Are you married but find that your "sex switch" is off? What from your past or in your present has caused you to turn off sexually?

- Do you want God to turn your switch on again? Why?

If you're single, you might think this doesn't apply to you. After all, you're saving sex for marriage so your switch *should* stay off. Right? Whether you're married or single, God has created us as women—sexual women. This does not change based on whether we're having sex or not. If you're single and desire to be married one day and experience a godly sexual relationship, I don't want you to turn your sexual switch off. I want you to trust God to help you direct it in a healthy and godly way until you are married. At the root of sexual desire is a cry for true intimacy. Sexual intimacy in marriage doesn't fulfill this underlying need, it enhances it. Discover now how to fulfill your true intimacy needs and not only will you be more attractive to a lifetime partner, but you'll become a healthier partner in return. Read some great books on being single and sexual like *Your Single Treasure* by Rick Stedman, or *Gift-Wrapped by God* and *Intimate Issues* by Lorraine Pintus and Linda Dillow.

Whether you realize it or not, your sexual past has shaped how you feel about sex today. It's just as important for you as a single woman as it is for a married woman to discover how your past sexual relationships have skewed your view of sex, otherwise your wrong views will follow you into your future marriage. If you don't examine it now, once you're married you may be surprised to discover that even though now your *body* can say yes to sex, your *mind* can't.

As you begin to read through the Song of Songs, remember to ask God to show you one or more verses or truths that are just for you today. Then ask Him how these truths apply to you specifically.

As you read, I want you to focus on some characteristics of the beloved's sexual attitude:[25]

She is responsive sexually to her husband. (4:16)

She is adventurous sexually. She not only responds to her husband's desire, but often initiates sexual pleasure with her husband. She often plans the romantic get-away for sex. (7:11-13)

She is uninhibited sexually. (7:1-3)

She is expressive with praise to her husband. (1:16, 2:3, 2:16)

She is sensuous. She daydreams about her husband's body and about their lovemaking. (5:10-16)

- Read the entire book of Song of Songs. What verse or truth stands out for you today?

- How does this new truth impact you today? Is there something about yourself, sex, others or God that He wants you to see differently?

Read Song of Songs 3:5.

If you have the *New American Standard Bible,* you will notice that the lover is the one quoting this verse. If you have the *New International Version* of the Bible, it attributes this phrase to the beloved. So who really said this? I'm not sure, but I love what Pastor Scott Bell shared on this topic from his sermon series on sex. He believes the Song is divided into various stages of a romantic relationship: attraction, dating, courtship, wedding and marriage. During the dating period in chapter two and the courtship in the beginning of chapter three, the lover protects his future wife's purity by not awakening her sexual desire too soon. He puts the brakes on the physical relationship before marriage.

I wonder how many of us as women used our sexuality to seduce our husbands or boyfriends before marriage, only to turn around after we've been married to feel distrust or resentment for their lack of strength to resist us then. Is that you? It was me. And that's what I felt. I used my sexuality to turn him on before marriage, but later in our marriage I used it against him.

Have you been with men who neglected to protect your purity? What, if any, was your role in this? (If you were sexually abused or raped, your sexual purity was robbed from you and was not your fault).

- How has that impacted your attitude towards men now?

- If you had sex with your husband before marriage, how do you think that may be impacting your relationship today? Emotionally and physically?

If you haven't already, ask God to forgive you for your part in losing your purity, and forgive your past partners' for their part in not protecting your purity.

Day Four: Song of Songs Part IV

"I am pleased to introduce Mr. and Mrs. King Solomon!" I can almost hear the Priest announce at the end of chapter three, concluding the marriage ceremony of Solomon and his bride. Now for the steamy sex part, chapter four--the wedding night. It begins with Solomon undressing his bride, and ends with the consummation of their marriage.

Once again, I want you to read the entire book, but as you do spend some extra time meditating on chapter four. Remember to ask God to show you one or more verses or truths that are just for you today. Then ask Him how these truths apply to you specifically.

- Read the entire book of Song of Songs. What verse or truth stands out for you?

- How does this new truth impact you? Is there something about yourself, sex, others or God that He wants you to see differently?

- Read Song of Songs 4:1-7. Notice that Solomon begins at the top of his bride and moves down with his adoring praises. Which part of the description stands out for you? Why?

- Solomon loves everything about his bride. When was the last time someone loved you like that?

- Who was it?

Did you know that God sees every part of you--your appearance, your personality, your gifts, your heart, and loves—is absolutely crazy about you? Every part of you. Why don't you take a moment and ask God to show you what He loves about you so much. Ask Him for a list like Solomon gave his bride. Write it here:

In Chapter 4:12-15, Solomon is describing the beauty of his beloved's virginity. He says that she's been saving her "garden" (virginity) for him. He describes it as a fragrant garden waiting to be opened, a fountain that has been sealed, waiting to flow to him.

Did anyone ever tell you that your purity and virginity was something so beautiful, so life-giving and fragrant that you needed to protect and treasure it? Save it for your future husband to open? No one told me. So I failed to treasure it, and I didn't expect others to treasure it either.

If we didn't treasure our sexual gift before we gave it away so carelessly or had it taken from us, it will be hard to see it now as something to treasure. But it still is. In 4:15 Solomon says that his beloved's sexual love is like a garden fountain, a well of flowing water streaming down—never ending throughout their marriage.

- Read Chapter 4:12-15. Do you see your sexual love as life-giving to your husband or future husband?

Can you imagine that every time you invite your husband to drink from your fountain and romp in your garden you're filling his soul with life-giving peace, love and joy that will overflow and fill you, your home and family? Ask God to change your mind about your garden of sex. The enemy has convinced you that it's been trashed--it's ugly and dirty, not beautiful. This is a lie! Your garden of sex is a fragrant, life-giving fountain, and you're the only one who can offer your husband this soulful drink.

Is your fountain sealed, dried up? Then take heart from verse 16 of chapter 4. Shulamith has kept her fountain sealed until this moment. Then in verse 16 she calls her fountain to awaken, her garden to release its fragrance. Then she invites her husband into *his* garden to have a taste and take a drink.

Has your garden stopped growing? Your fountain no longer flowing? Ask God to turn your fountain on, make the flowers grow again, let the life-giving stream flow with abundance again. Then invite your husband to have a drink—in *his* garden. The garden God has given you to give to *him.*

If you're single, learn from Solomon's bride. She always *had* a growing garden but she kept it locked. She always *had* a flowing fountain but it stayed sealed--until God entrusted her to the one who was chosen to unlock it, to drink from it. The time to repair your garden and restore your fountain is now, not once you're married. Ask God to return life to your garden and a stream of life-giving water to your fountain and then entrust Him with the key until your wedding night.

Do you know that God wants you to have lots of sex when you're married? Don't believe me? Look at Chapter 5:1 under *Friends*: "Eat, O friends, and drink; drink your fill; O lovers." That is God telling the husband and wife to eat and drink their fill of each other sexually. Have you ever thought that God actually cares about your marital sex life? In fact He takes delight whenever we do what He created us to do--in this case, blessing each other with the gift of marital sex.

If God sees everything and is everywhere then He's there when you're having sex too—in marriage or out of marriage. He was there when you gave it away freely before marriage and when you had it taken from you, in abuse or rape. In marriage, He delights in what He sees. Outside marriage, His heart weeps for you.

Some of us took our 'fill' of sex outside marriage, and now in marriage we've *had* our fill. Is that you? Ask God to restore your desire to eat and drink and have your fill of each other in your marriage, or once you're married.

And remember, He's watching—with great delight.

Day Five: Song of Songs Part V

Five days of love and sex. Have you had enough? I hope not, because I've saved the best for last. This book is bulging with more truths than we have time for in this chapter, but I hope that your appetite for sex has been restored so you'll continue your study of God's book on sex. Another resource that I've found helpful as you decipher the truths in this book is *Intimacy Ignited*, by Dr. Joseph and Linda Dillow and Dr. Peter and Lorraine Pintus. It's great bed-time reading if you're married. If not, wait until you are and read it with your husband.

The last few chapters of Song of Songs deal with the dynamics of married life: how to handle conflict, how to treat your spouse, how to plan romantic encounters and how to stay madly in love as you grow old together. Sound good? Let's get started.

As you read through this book for the last time this week, ask God to show you one or more verses or truths that are just for you today. Then ask Him how these truths apply to you specifically. If you can, spend some extra time today meditating on this incredible book.

- Read the entire book of Song of Songs. What verse or truth stands out for you today?

- How does this new truth impact you? Is there something about yourself, sex, others or God that He wants you to see differently?

- Chapter five starts out with them fighting, see Chapter 5:2-3. Specifically, the new bride doesn't want to have sex. Sound familiar? What does Solomon do? (verse 5:6)

- How does she respond to Solomon's departure? (verse 5:6-8)

The beloved doesn't let conflict between them last. She pursues reconciliation even at personal cost. Then she reflects on the good qualities of her husband.

- Read Chapter 5:10-16. Do you often reflect on the positive characteristics of your husband, or do you gravitate to the ones that irritate you? What are your husband's good qualities? If you're single, what qualities are you looking for in a future husband?

Ask God to allow your thoughts to dwell more on your husband's good qualities rather than his annoying ones. After all, you may have a few annoying ones of your own, don't you? I know I do.

- Read Chapter 6:8-9. What is Solomon saying about his bride? Would you like your husband/boyfriend to see you like that? Do you see them like that? Does your spouse know that he is the most important person in the world to you? Why or why not?

- Read Chapter 7:1-6. This guy is good. In chapter four he describes her from the neck down, this time he's describing her from the feet up. How creative! What do you do to creatively show your love to your husband?

- What could you do tonight?

If you're single, how creative have you been in past relationships in regard to non-sexual or physical signs of love. Ask God to give you some creative ideas. Write them here.

- Read Chapter 7:11-13. What is the beloved planning here? How often do you make plans for five-star romance—either at home or away on a romantic retreat? When was the last time you did?

Start making plans today for the next time. Put it on the calendar. Write your plans here:

- Read Chapter 8:2. Who taught the beloved how to love her husband?

- Who taught you how to love men? What do you need to unlearn from your past lessons?

- What new lessons do you need to learn? Who will you ask to teach you?

- The climax of this whole book is Chapter 8:6-7. How is true love described? Does your love feel like this?

God is the one who gives us this kind of love. We can't conjure it up on our own. Ask God to give you this kind of love for your husband. Ask Him to make it a like a blazing fire that never goes out.

God puts this kind of love in our hearts but we must choose to love. Did you hear that? We won't feel love every day, but we can choose to love. The world tells us that when we're not feeling the love, we can move on. That's not what God says. His gift of love is just a prayer away. You can have it if you ask Him for it, and you can choose to offer it regardless of how you're feeling.

- Read Chapter 8:14. What is the beloved asking for? Reread Chapter 1:2. What was on her mind at the beginning of this book? What is similar?

Whether you're married or single God uses this love story to teach us His desire for us sexually. He shows us through the beloved how to be expressive, uninhibited and responsive in our love-making. He uses her example to remind us that our gardens are continually growing. And sex can be more fulfilling as we grow old together. Don't give in to the temptation that it's not necessary later in marriage. Solomon's bride takes the initiative to plan a romantic get-away often. She's creative, spontaneous and playful. She saves all her desire, thoughts, and seduction for her husband—no one else.

If you're single, God provides specific guidelines in dating, building relationships and courtship--specifically, not to awaken sexual desire before marriage. Solomon's bride looked for a man of godly character. One who would protect her purity and treasure her above his immediate desire. One who was strong but gentle. One who would put her first above himself. One who would love her with unconditional love.

Would someone like that fulfill your heart's desire? I'm sure it would, because God is the one who gave you those desires, so He knows how to fill them. Pray and ask God to give you a man like that. Ask Him to help you wait for such a man, and have the eyes to recognize him when you see him.

This could be discouraging if you're married. Maybe your man doesn't have the character of Solomon. Maybe he hasn't honored you or treasured you or loved you the way you'd hoped. There's still hope! God can repair, restore and resurrect anything—a man, a woman and a marriage. But I guarantee, He won't start with your man—He'll start with you. Ask Him to begin to change you and watch how it changes your man.

Think About It…

- What's the most significant truth you've learned this week? Write out the verse (if applicable) that God used to speak to you.

- What is God asking you to do with this new truth?

- Write out your response (prayer) to God here:

CHAPTER ELEVEN

Breaking Free

Day One: Broken Heart

Back in Chapter Six, lesson three, I talked briefly about a hardened and broken heart. I asked you to indicate on a line where your heart was. Do you remember? Well today I'd like to elaborate on the difference between a proud heart and a broken heart.

During your quiet time with God read through this list from Nancy Leigh DeMoss[26] and ask Him to reveal where your heart is. Place a check on the sentences that apply to you—whether they are on the proud or broken side. We'll all have checkmarks on both sides of this chart. What you want to look for is which side has the most checkmarks. That will be an indication of how your heart operates.

It will be enlightening as well as humbling. Use the remainder of your time asking God to begin to change your heart by first breaking it and then allowing Him to heal your brokenness. If you recall in my story, this was the prayer that God used to show me who I really was, who and what I trusted in and how I treated others. It was powerful—but it was also painful. I'll be praying for you as you open your heart to Him.

Start with this prayer from Psalm 139:23-24:

"Search me O God, and know my heart; test me and know my anxious thoughts. See if there is any offensive way in me, and lead me in the way of righteousness."

Proud People	Broken People
Focus on the failures of others	Overwhelmed with a sense of their own spiritual need
Self-righteous; look down on others	Esteem all others better than themselves
Independent, self-sufficient spirit	Have a dependent spirit; recognize their need for others
Have to prove that they are right	Willing to yield the right to be right
Claim rights, have a demanding spirit	Yield their rights; have a meek spirit
Desire to be served	Motivated to serve others
Desire to be a success	Motivated to be faithful and to make others a success
Desire self-advancement	Desire to promote others
Wounded when others get promoted and they are overlooked	Eager for others to get the credit; rejoice when others are lifted up
Feel confident in how much they know	Humbled by how very much they have to learn
Self conscious	Not concerned with self at all
Unapproachable or defensive when criticized	Receive criticism with a humble, open spirit
Want to be sure that no one finds out when they have sinned, their instinct is to cover up	Once broken, don't care who knows or who finds out, are willing to be exposed because they have nothing to lose.
Remorseful over their sin, sorry that they got found out or caught	Truly, genuinely repentant over their sin, evidenced in the fact that they forsake that sin
Wait for the other to come and ask forgiveness when there is a misunderstanding or conflict in a relationship	Take the initiative to be reconciled when there is misunderstanding or conflict in relationships, they race to the cross; they see if they can get there first, no matter how wrong the other may have been
Compare themselves with others and feel worthy of honor	Compare themselves to the holiness of God and feel a desperate need for His mercy

During your prayer time with God ask Him to show you attitudes, thoughts, words or actions that you need to confess and ask forgiveness for. Are there some people that God is bringing to mind that you need to ask forgiveness from? Make a list. If you can call them—do so. If you need to write a letter—there's no better time. I had to do both when I first went through this. Actually, I'm still doing it--whenever God brings someone to mind that I've spoken unkindly about, or to, or…that reminds me—there's a letter I've been meaning to write…

Don't be afraid of brokenness. It's our greatest strength. God constantly reminds us that it's in our weakness and brokenness that His power, strength and glory shine the brightest. Jesus was not afraid to be broken for us. He came into the world broken, He left it broken. There is no greater honor than to be broken for Him. Psalm 34:18 says, *"The LORD is close to the brokenhearted and saves those who are crushed in spirit."* And one of my all-time favorites is Isaiah 66:2: *"This is the one I esteem: (declares the LORD), he who is humble and contrite in spirit and trembles at my word."*

There you have it. God delights in brokenness. He esteems, is close to and "lifts up" the humble and brokenhearted, James 4:10 says.

If brokenness brings me closer to God—then I pray, bring it on, O LORD.

Day Two: Step One – Surrender

Are you eating humble pie today? Or does it feel like someone threw the whole pie in your face? I'm sorry. You were probably starting to feel better about yourself until yesterday, but today you're not so sure again. Don't despair. If you're feeling broken today then you're exactly where you need to be. You're in the right place. Because a broken heart is willing to do something a proud heart isn't—it's willing to give up. Yes, give up—surrender, submit relinquish everything to God. And if you want to heal and grow, then it starts right here.

By giving up.

It may seem a little late in the study to address this because the fact that you've gotten this far means you've already been surrendering yourself to God. Little by little, week by week you've been giving God access to the things you've been holding onto all these years. You've been letting go of your past, your present and your future and giving God control. Right? In fact this entire study has been an exercise of surrender.

But after yesterday's exercise you may be wondering if there are still some areas that you haven't surrendered completely to God. You're probably right, because wherever there is pride, there is no surrender. Pride compels us to hold on tight, surrender lets go. Let me illustrate.

Hold out your hands, palms up. Now close your fists tightly. This is what pride does. It causes us to be self-focused and closed off. This causes us stress. Look at your fingers and wrist when you're squeezing your palms tightly closed. See how tight and stretched they look? How long could you keep that position? Not long. Your hands and wrists will soon get tired from the stress put on the muscles. That's what pride does to us. We strive, strain, defend and hide, because we must at all costs 'look okay, or great, or better.' It's exhausting isn't it? The more we strive the worse we feel, so the more we're compelled to strive. Sound familiar?

Now, open your palms. This is a broken heart. It's open, inviting, vulnerable and relaxed. See your hands and wrists. No stress—no strain. A broken heart is at peace just like your palms. A broken heart has no defense—it knows it's broken. It doesn't strive to appear whole and put-together because it acknowledges that it's broken. And here's the best news. God inhabits the hearts of the broken and surrendered. Isaiah 57:15 says: *"I live in a high and holy place, but also with him who is contrite and lowly in spirit, to revive the spirit of the lowly and to revive the heart of the contrite."* Once there, He heals that broken, surrendered heart. And then he sets that heart free to grow. Free to become all He created it to be.

So, what are you still holding on to? What is God showing you that you've yet to surrender completely to Him?

If there's one thing I'm learning on this adventure with God, it's that surrendering is a process—one that needs to happen daily. And every day as I surrender my heart to Him, He shows me new areas that I've yet to surrender, unaware that I was still holding on to. So, when you to surrender everything to God, be willing to let Him have *everything*. Then respond with 'yes' when He shows you specific areas He wants you to let go of. And don't worry, with God it will be one thing at a time. One attitude, one person, one habit, one lie at a time. Thank goodness we have a lifetime. And praise God, He's not in a hurry with us.

- Read 2 Chronicles 7:14. How is surrender described in this verse?

- What are the results when we surrender to God?

- Read James 4:7-10. These verses describe submission to God in action. How are we to submit to God in these verses?

- What is the result when we submit ourselves to God?

There are two people God wants us to submit to: first Him, and then others. In fact, submission to God naturally overflows into submission to others. Look at this verse:

Ephesians 5:21. To whom should we submit? Who are we submitting to others for?

Does this seem like a tricky question? The answer is: God wants us to submit to each other. Husbands are to submit to their wives, wives to their husbands, fellow Christians are to submit to each other, we are to submit to authority, children to their parents, and so on. A heart surrendered to Christ makes it possible to submit to others in our lives. Why? Because whether I'm the leader or the follower, my surrendered heart compels me to serve and love others. That means putting aside my selfish desires for the good of others. If you're having trouble submitting to others in your life, I would examine how surrendered your heart is to God. The more surrendered I am to God, the more submissive I become in my relationships. That's how it works.

So we are to submit to others, but who are we doing it for? For Christ. Why? *Because others aren't always deserving of our submission*--certainly not our husbands, our bosses, the government. You get the picture. If I wait to submit to others until they deserve it, it would never happen. So we are to submit to others for Christ--because He first submitted to us. Remember, He was God—but gave all that up to be our servant. He is the perfect, selfless example of submission.

So next time you're tempted not to submit to someone because they don't deserve it, remember you didn't deserve it either, but Jesus did it anyways.

- Who is it easier to submit to, God or others? If it's others, who in particular?

- If you're finding it hard to submit to others, ask God what that has to do with being willing to submit to Him. There will be a direct connection.

Day Three: Break the Silence

Your life is your story. Yet we all have things in our past and present that we'd rather not share. In fact, there are pieces we wish weren't part of our story. We'd like to put those things in a box and store it far back in the closet of our souls and pretend that it has nothing to do with who we are today. But I'm sorry—it's just not true. Everything that's happened from your birth on has shaped who you are today.

I clearly remember the day God revealed this to me. I was sitting in my closet-sanctuary reading *The Purpose Driven Life*, by Rick Warren. Chapter 31 was called "Understanding Your Shape." I was reading about how my past experiences had shaped and molded me—something I knew as a behavioral psychology major. But then I read that God uses the painful experiences in our past more than any other experiences--the ones we resent and regret, hide and deny, to prepare us for our greatest ministry in helping others. What? I couldn't believe what I was reading. In fact, Warren says that these past painful experiences, "They *are* your ministry." Warren goes on to say, "For God to use your painful experiences, you must be willing to share them. You have to stop covering them up, and you must honestly admit your faults, failures and fears."[27] This was really scary to me.

All these years I'd been hiding my past—and now God was telling me they were my greatest ministry? "No thank you," was my first reaction. You see I had convinced myself that my past had nothing to do with who I was today. That was so yesterday—I was not the same person. It had no impact on me today, or on my ministry. But like an audible voice, a clear thought came into my mind that I knew was God speaking. "Barb, your past has everything to do with who you are today. It shapes how you feel, how you think, and what you're passionate about. I want you to give me your past."

For a second, my heart said "no". I knew giving God my past meant I'd have to share it. I wasn't necessarily thinking about writing a book on it, leading Bible studies, or speaking around the country on it. Thank goodness, or I might still be saying no. I just knew I'd have to start being open about it to my family, my children, my church. That was scary enough. Thankfully, my no was just for a second. Then I knew I had to—I wanted to. I *longed to.* My heart sensed that God was offering me something so much better than what I was living. I was exhausted trying to cover it up, and I wanted to be free. I gave God my past that day. I sat there with my palms open and up as a symbol to God that He could have all of me—not just my acceptable parts, but my ugly ones too. I knew He didn't just want the 'Sunday-best' me, but the *real* me--my past, my pain, my shame, my secret. It was His now to do whatever He wanted. Contrary to the lies, God had no intention of punishing me, shaming me or condemning me. He wanted to love and heal me, and take away all the shame and pain. Then He would give it back to me as my ministry so I could offer it to others.

As He did, something amazing happened. He didn't have to make me tell others—I wanted to. I shared without realizing it. And when I did, there was no more shame. Why not? Because breaking the silence diffuses the lie and breaks its hold on us. Take a moment and read the first page of Chapter One from *The Invisible Bond.*

- What has keeping secrets done to you? Your family? Your spiritual life?

- You've begun to share your story in this group, or to your support person. How has that made you feel?

- How has telling your story defeated and diffused the enemy's lies in your life?

- What truth do you now see that you didn't when you kept quiet?

But be careful. While you're in the vulnerable healing process it's important that you trust God before you share your story. Not everyone is safe. Some people will not offer grace and acceptance, but rejection and judgment. Maybe you've already experienced that. I know I did. Early on I was criticized, even persecuted, by people in the church and my extended family for my divorce. That convinced me that no one, especially those in the church, could ever know the full truth about me. In my mind the divorce was the least serious of my sins. If that was causing such condemnation, imagine what wrath the 'biggies' would incur. The enemy used that lie to keep me quiet for the next twenty-five years. I don't want that to happen to you. Your group and your support person are safe people to share your story with. But ask God's direction before you share it with others. I found that whenever I felt God leading me to share my story, the recipient was either hurting just like me and it was exactly what they needed to hear, or they had something to share that I needed to hear.

Once you've experienced healing and the enemy's tactics of shame don't work anymore, you'll be free to share your story with anyone, because then it will no longer be about you—

it will be about what God has done in your life. Then if others reject you, you'll realize that it's God they're rejecting, not you.

Spend some time today reading Mark 5:24-34.

- Jesus calls the woman out of the crowd to share her story. Why does He do that?

- Verse 33 says the woman falls at His feet in fear and tells him the *whole* story. God already knows her whole story, so why is it important for her to tell Him?

- Who else would have heard her story?

- What are some of the results of the woman having her secret exposed?

- What does Jesus do for her? Physically? Spiritually? Relationally? Emotionally?

Jesus is calling you out of the crowd too. The rest of the crowd is still keeping their stories a secret. But you have answered His call to come forward and share your *whole* story. Now as you go out and share what God has done, you'll be able to offer those in your 'crowd' the courage to come and fall at Jesus' feet too.

And then you'll have your new ministry.

Day Four: Praying the Prayer

Today's the day. The day to do something with the sexual history list you've been making since the beginning of this study. If you haven't finished making your list than you'll need to do that before you can move into this very important step. Please resist the urge—I know you feel it—to skip this part. Yes, you've been in this study for quite awhile now and you've begun to experience some wonderful healing and victory. But this prayer was instrumental in God completely severing the sexual bonds I'd made in my past. And it will be for you as well.

So take a deep breath. Make plans to have some extended time in a quiet, undistracted place. Put on some soft Christian music if you want and get ready for a spiritual adventure. In preparation for this exercise, please read the entire sixth chapter in the *Invisible Bond* or Chapter Seven in *Kiss Me Again*. This is where you'll find the steps to help prepare you to say the prayer.

Once you've read through the chapter, get out your list. Ask God if there is anyone else you need to add to your list before you begin. Take your time. Ask God to show you what you need to see in this exercise. Ask Him for godly sorrow rather than worldly sorrow as you pray. If you rush through it, you'll most likely have to do it again.

When I prayed through my list I didn't feel anything at the beginning. There was no lightening, no sudden earth movements, no great spiritual revelations. But as I reached the half-way point in my list, God broke through my monotonous recitation with new insight. As clearly as if it was written on my paper I saw what God saw. I saw my part—my offense against them. Outwardly they may have seemed the greatest offenders, but inwardly I had been driven to use them from impure and selfish motives. What I had done was wrong. Using them was wrong. Misusing God's gift of sex was wrong. Denying God the opportunity to fulfill my need for love and acceptance was heartbreaking to Him. For the first time ever, I felt His sadness. He was hurt—by me. *I* had hurt *Him*.

My prayer for the second half of my list was very different from the first half--because now I was weeping. My sorrow was real. It was no longer a nice little exercise. It became a divine experience, a supernatural transformation of my mind—from how *I* saw things to how they really were in God's view.

So guess what I did? When I finished my list, I started back at the top. I may have said the words for the top half, but now I wanted to mean them with all my heart. And just like Peter 4:1 says, my suffering allowed me to be done with my sin—and my list.

The bonds were broken, the ties were cut. Forever. Praise God.

Let's begin:

1. Ask God to bring to mind everyone with whom you've had sexual contact, or created a bond with—voluntarily or involuntarily. Wait quietly, allowing God to bring names, faces, or events to memory.

2. Write down each name. If you don't know the name, write a description of the person or event.

3. Ask God to help you see your sin with His eyes.

4. Pray that your heart will be humbled and your spirit contrite, so that you will experience true repentance.

5. Pray the prayer below (or something like it) for each name or incident on your list.

Note: If you became bonded through rape or sexual abuse, omit the part in the prayer asking God to forgive you of your violation against the other person; you were an innocent victim and had no intention of violating or defrauding him or her in this manner (see 1 Thessalonians 4:6). But you do need to forgive that person for violating you. And you need to ask God to sever the bonds you have inadvertently created with that person.

Lord, I ask forgiveness for sinning against You and against my own body. In the name of Jesus Christ, I sever and renounce the bonds I created with _____. *In the name of Jesus, I release my heart tie with this person physically, emotionally, and spiritually. I choose by faith to forgive* _____ *for the violation against me. I also ask for forgiveness of my violation of him (or her). Please remove the negative emotional baggage that I have been carrying around with me, by which I have been harming others. Restore to me a virgin heart, as though I had never been with this person, and heal me completely of the damage this sin has caused my body, my soul, and my spirit. I accept your forgiveness, and I reject the enemy's attack—his attempts to fill me with shame associated with this person. I claim complete healing and restoration in the name of Jesus. Amen.*"[28]

Day Five: Forsaking the Past

"Since we have these promises, dear friends, let us purify ourselves from everything that contaminates body and spirit, perfecting holiness out of reverence for God." 2 Corinthians 7:1

People often want to know exactly what I did to break the bonds with my past sexual partners. They want a 'one-two-three' answer they can follow to achieve the same results. I'm sorry to tell you it doesn't work that way. We're individuals with different personalities and experiences. We learn differently. We even relate to God differently. He's the same God—but we're all different. What God uses to teach or convict me, make me laugh or cry will be different from what He uses to move you. That's one of the things I love about God. There are things we can do to help our healing progress and be successful, but how and when it happens will be different for each of us. Because we're not in control—God is.

Writing your sexual history list and praying for God to break the bonds is an essential piece of the healing journey—but it's only one piece. We are spiritual beings, but we are also physical and emotional beings. The bond of sex involves all these unique parts of us and so the healing must include them all as well.

The various activities throughout this Bible study have allowed God to change you. Writing anger and forgiveness letters, writing your sexual history list and praying through it have been tools to allow God to do the work in you. Today's list includes practical steps you can take that will eliminate the physical reminders and triggers of your past sexual partners—and even present sexual partners or struggles. Again God does the miracle work in us, but this is our part in the process.

So what does it mean to get rid of physical reminders? From past relationships you've collected items that have created memories for you of this person: music, letters, cards, jewelry, pictures, gifts, clothes, email addresses, phone numbers, etc. Part of the process of breaking the sexual bond to them, will be removing these tangible reminders that keep their memory alive. For whatever reason, physical reminders can trigger memories and dreams of past lovers, keeping the attachment alive. I'm not sure why this step is important, I just know it is. And I know that God uses this step to completely sever the sexual bonds with past partners.

This can be the hardest step. We're willing to go through the self-examination, work through the painful memories, even make ourselves vulnerable to others, but often the part we resist the most is forsaking things in the present that allow Satan to trigger memories of the past. Melanie, a woman from one of my sexual healing groups was resisting this step. She had a large orange trunk out in the garage that held mementos of her earlier life—the one she was asking God to heal. But having lost the key to the trunk, she decided not to worry about this step. But on this day in the study as she prayed for God to show her the tangible reminders He wanted her to remove, something miraculous happened. Something only God could do. As she casually cleaned out a drawer in her bathroom, she came across a small cloth bag. Inside the bag was the key to her trunk! I guess God thought it was important after all!

For those of you asking God to sever a bond with an ex-husband with whom you've had children, some exceptions may apply. For example, if you have wedding pictures, and pictures of your ex-husband with your children, you will want to keep these for your children's sake. There may also be gifts your husband has given you, as in jewelry, etc., that you'd like to pass down to your children one day. If you're sharing custody with your ex-husband you also can't remove his contact information from your phone, or him from your life. In this case, God is faithful to help you sever the spiritual and emotional and even chemical bond you've created with him even though he may continue to be a part of your life. Pray and ask God what physical reminders are appropriate to eliminate, and which ones you should keep. He'll show you.

Unfortunately God's healing work in our life can be inhibited if we're not willing to take this important step. In addition to removing past reminders, there may be people, places and activities you're still associating with that keep the past alive, or continue to wound you in the present. We can't experience healing or break sexual bonds when we're continuing to participate in the very activities that have wounded us in the first place, or continue to create a bond with us. We will never heal from something as long as we're continuing to re-wound ourselves. Nor will we be completely free from our memories if we have items from the past that trigger them.

Read over the following list and ask God to show you what you need to forsake. He may reveal something that isn't on my list that needs to be on yours.

- If you're not married and having sex, whether it's with a long time boyfriend or casual partners, you need to stop, now.

- If you're in a co-habiting relationship with someone of the opposite sex who is not your spouse, one of you needs to move out.

- If you've had several relationship failures in your past, consider taking a break from dating or getting involved in a romantic relationship for a certain amount of time. I've had women tell me they've made a commitment to themselves and God to give up dating for six months, even a year, as they allow God to heal them from past wounds.

- If you're married or in a serious relationship and considering marriage, break off any ties with past lovers—remove their email addresses and phone numbers from your contacts. Continuing a 'friendship' with a past lover is impossible if you want to completely break the sexual bond you've created with them.

- Go through your house and remove any items that remind you of past lovers. Notes, cards, letters, pictures and gifts all need to go.

- Put 2 Corinthians 10:3-5 into practice by "taking every thought captive and making it obedient to Christ." Satan will continue to try to bring your past lovers to your mind. As I've said before, this is not the sin but the temptation. What you do with that thought can become sin. If you continue to dwell on the thought it can lead to sin. Tell God you take that thought captive and give it to Him. Ask Him to replace that thought with His truth.

- Ask God to show you what are you watching, reading or listening to that triggers thoughts of past lovers. Movies, soap operas, magazines, sexual songs or romance novels can ignite thoughts of your past.

- Ask God to reveal unhealthy friends in your life. Do your current friends support you in your desire for purity? Are they also attempting to live pure lives? Or just the opposite? If so, pray and ask God to bring godly friends into your life, and start to distance yourself from friends who do not share your values.

- What activities do you participate in that may contribute to your failure? If alcohol has been involved in your past sexual relationships, consider reducing or eliminating your intake. Evaluate the places you frequent; i.e., are you into the bar scene where drinking and sexual immorality can be a temptation?

- If married, are you becoming emotionally connected with someone of the opposite sex who is not your spouse? If you're single, this can be dangerous if that person is married. Emotional affairs usually lead to physical affairs. If that is happening to you, break contact with that person immediately. Guard your heart and mind from going down this path.

- What is God revealing to you from this list that you need to forsake or change in your life? Write it below:

- What are you going to do with what God's revealed to you today?

The following verse was written at the beginning of today's lesson. Read it out loud. The list I've given you are examples of some of the contaminates this verse is talking about, but maybe there's something else that God wants to reveal to you that's not on my list.

"Since we have these promises, dear friends, let us purify ourselves from everything that contaminates body and spirit, perfecting holiness out of reverence for God" (2 Corinthians 7:1).

As you meditate on this verse, pray and ask God to show you if there is anything else contaminating your mind, body or spirit and keeping you from being completely free from your past.

Now the hard part—putting into practice what God has revealed to you today. You may be willing, but you have no idea how to begin. Or you may need accountability to follow through with it. Enlist the help of your leaders, support person or pastor if moving from revelation to execution is a challenge. At the least, let them know what you're doing so they can support you and be praying for you.

Think About It…

- What's the most significant truth you've learned this week? Write out the verse (if applicable) that God used to speak to you.

- What is God asking you to do with this new truth?

- Write out your response (prayer) to God here:

CHAPTER TWELVE

Healing for the Long-Term

"For I know the plans I have for you,' declares the LORD, *'plans to prosper you and not to harm you, plans to give you hope and a future'"* Jeremiah 29:11.

Day One: A New View of You

God has begun something brand *new* in you. Can you feel it? He plucked you off the path you were on and headed you in a new direction. Can you see it? He's given you a new purpose, a new destiny, a new ministry. Have you discovered what it is?

God loves to *exceed* our expectations—every time. What did you come to God for at the beginning of this study? What did you ask Him for? Whatever it was, I know that when we humble ourselves before God, James 4:10 says He delights in lifting us up—beyond our wildest imagination. He loves to answer prayers we never prayed, and give us things we didn't even know to ask for. That's the God we have—the one we humble ourselves before.

This week we're going to look at how God has changed our view of everything—ourselves, sex, God, others. For some, the changes have been obvious and you're already rejoicing in what God has done. Maybe you've been working through healing from several things in your past—abuse, rape, abortion, etc., and this has been a final step in your journey. Although you haven't 'arrived', you're feeling more complete, more whole than you've ever felt.

For others, the changes have been more subtle, not so obvious, and you're wondering if you've really made significant strides. Don't despair. I thought the same until I reflected on how I felt when I began the study to when I finished--the changes were stunning. My healing happened slowly, internally and I didn't realize my inner transformation was being reflected on the outside until God had me look back.

Then there are some that may feel like this study has stirred up more painful issues than you knew you had. "Great," you're thinking. "Now I have more things to work on." Once again, don't despair. I've discovered that God heals us slowly, one issue at a time. Although many of us have had wounding from various circumstances, God will often bring just one to the surface. Once we learn to trust Him with that issue and we experience freedom, we are able to see what else we need to release to God. If God led you here first but now you've discovered there is more for you to work on, praise God! Although that may be discouraging, it's proof of His relentless love for you. He won't be content with your partial healing and freedom—and neither should you.

Remember, this is not a race—there is no deadline. This is *your* journey with God—not mine, nor anyone else's. You have no one else to keep up to—just God. Don't be discouraged if you're not done yet. Be thankful that God has you on this path and no matter how long it takes, He's never going to leave you or give up on you. If you feel like giving up right now, I'm actually excited for you. Yes, you heard me correctly.

I'm thrilled for you.

Something wonderful is about to happen. I've discovered that when we're feeling the greatest discouragement, a breakthrough is just around the corner. We're about to experience something so incredible, so bondage-breaking that the enemy is desperate to keep us on this side of the pain—the defeated side. He *never* wants you to be free. If you're at your most desperate, defeated moment, please be encouraged. Recognize what's happening. God is about to set you free and the enemy is fighting to keep you imprisoned. Don't let him. Push through the pain, ignore the urge to quit. Freedom, healing and victory are closer than you think—moments, just steps away. Just hang on.

Regardless of how much healing you think you've experienced, you've changed—inside and out. At the beginning of this study you filled out some sheets to help you determine what you were struggling with as a result of your sexual past. (or if you're doing this in a group, you may have done this during an intake interview). Today I want you to fill out two of them again—the symptom checklist and the current status assessment sheet. At the end of today's lesson are the two sheets. Please fill them out now.

Once you've completed both sheets, get the same two sheets from the beginning of this study and compare your answers from the beginning of the study to now. Make a note of how your answers have changed.

Symptom Checklist: Make a list of the changes you see in your two lists.

- What is your most significant change according to this sheet?

Current Status Assessment: Make a list of the changes you see in this sheet.

- What change is the most significant according to this sheet?

- What was your greatest struggle or symptom before you started this study?

- How would you rate it then on a scale of 1-10 (10 being the greatest)?

- How would you rate it now?

- Is there something that was not a struggle for you prior to the study that has become one now? What is it? Why do you think this symptom has surfaced?

- What symptom did you not experience significant healing from that you wanted to?

- Because we're on a journey towards healing, what are you still trusting God to heal in you as you move forward?

- Go back and review Chapter Three of this study. How did you view yourself then?

- How do you see yourself now? To what do you attribute the change?

- How has your view of how God sees you changed since the beginning of this study?

Reflect on the following verses as you finish today's lesson.

Who I am in Christ.[29] The Word of God says **I am**:

- Created in the image of God by Him (Genesis 1:26-27; Psalm 119:73; Psalm 139:13-16)

- Chosen (Deuteronomy 7: 6-8; John 15:16; Ephesians 1:4; 1 Thessalonians 1:4; 1 Peter 2:9)

- Protected by God (Deuteronomy 33:12, 27; Joshua 1:3-9; Isaiah 43:1-5)

- Forgiven (Colossians 1:14; Hebrews 9:14; 1 John 1:9; 1 John 2:12)

- Blessed (Psalm 1:1-3; Psalm 65:4; Ephesians 1:3)

- The 'apple of God's eye' (Deuteronomy 32:10;Psalm 17:8)

- Washed clean from my sins (Isaiah 1:18; Ezekiel 36:25)

- Always in God's thoughts (Psalm 139:17,18; Isaiah 49:15,16; Jeremiah 29:11)

- Loved by God (Jeremiah 31:3; Romans 8:37-39; Ephesians 3:17-19; 1 John 4:16-19)

- Valued by God (Matthew 10:29-31)

- The temple of the Holy Spirit (1 Corinthians 6:19-20)

- A new creation in Christ (2 Corinthians 5:17)

- Redeemed from the curse of the law (Galatians 3:13)

- Set free (John 8:31-32)

- More than a conqueror (Romans 8:37)

- Sealed with the Holy Spirit (Ephesians 1:13-14)

- In Christ Jesus (1 Corinthians 1:30)

- Complete in Him (Colossians 2:9-10)

- Free from condemnation (Romans 8:1)

- Reconciled to God (2 Corinthians 5:18)

- Called of God (2 Timothy 1:9)

• Which one is the most significant for you?

Symptom Check List[30]

Use the same 0-3 rating as before.   Date:

	After Study
Have Difficulty Expressing Yourself Sexually	
Avoid times of intimacy	
Anxiety/Panic/Nervous Tension	
Feeling Numb (esp. during sex)	
Grief/Loss/Sorrow/Sadness	
Regret/Guilt/Shame	
Loneliness/Isolation/Difficulty Making friends	
Feeling "Branded" - As If Other People Can Tell	
Alienation/Feeling Different from Other People	
Depression/Hopelessness	
Have a General Mistrust of Men or Women	
Inability to Trust Myself or My Decisions/Self Doubt	
Anger/Rage	
Feelings of Having Been Victimized	
Feel Powerless to Assert /Protect Yourself against Sexual Harm	
Fear of Punishment	
Dreams/Nightmares/Difficulty Sleeping	
Fear or Discomfort with Sex or with Sexuality	
Seasons or Cycles of Depression/Sickness/or Accident Prone	
Flashbacks or Hallucinations related to past experiences	
Difficulty Concentrating	
Secrecy/Difficulty Telling Others about Past	
Difficulty forgetting and/or difficulty remembering past sexual incidents	
Feeling 'Crazy'	
Crying Too Much or Too Easily/Inability to Cry	
Difficulty Bonding with or Overprotective of Children	
Do you struggle with eating too much or too little	
Increased Drug or Alcohol Use/Addiction	
Need to use Alcohol/Drugs to engage/enjoy sex	
Suicidal Thoughts/Attempts	
Fatigue/Tiredness	
Marital Difficulties/Marital Stress	
Need to be in Control	
Promiscuity (Many Sexual Partners)	
Feel Unworthy of Being Loved/Cared for	
Struggle with feelings of lust	
Are you tempted with Sexual Perversions	
Have Self Punishing Behaviors	
Struggle with Desiring /Enjoying Sex with Your Spouse	
Need to fantasize or use pornography to be sexually aroused	
Lowered Self-worth/Inferiority	
Struggle with Self/Other Contempt/Condemnation	

CURRENT STATUS ASSESSMENT

Date: _____

Have you experienced any of the following (check all that apply):

_____ Schizophrenia	_____ Depression	_____ Mood Swings
_____ Anxiety/Panic Attacks	_____ Suicide or Attempts	_____ Sexual Abuse
_____ Physical Abuse	_____ Alcohol Abuse	_____ Imprisonment
_____ Learning Disability	_____ Attention Deficit	_____ Drug Abuse
_____ Dementia/Brain Damage	_____ Adoption	_____ Abortion
_____ Viewing Pornography	_____ Baby born out of wedlock	
_____ Extra-Marital Affairs	_____ Cutting or Self Destructive Behaviors	

SYMPTOM & PROBLEM LIST
PLEASE CHECK THOSE THAT YOU ARE EXPERIENCING NOW

_____ No Energy	_____ Mood Swings	_____ Distractible
_____ Cannot Enjoy Life	_____ Unusual Experiences	_____ Sexual Indiscretions
_____ Memory Problems	_____ Physical Numbness	_____ Socially Withdrawn
_____ Anxiety	_____ Panic Attacks	_____ Eating Disorder
_____ Fatigue	_____ Vomiting	_____ Alcohol Use
_____ Anger Outbursts	_____ Drug Use	_____ Unsure of Reality
_____ Shortness of Breath	_____ Insomnia	_____ Wishing to Die
_____ Reliving Past Events	_____ Disturbing Memories	_____ Confusing
_____ No Loving Feelings	_____ Low Self-Esteem	_____ Weight Change
_____ Fears	_____ Poor Appetite	_____ Depressed
_____ Decisions Difficult	_____ Headache	_____ Guilt Feelings
_____ Racing Thoughts	_____ Flashbacks	_____ Poor Concentration
_____ Hard to Make Friends	_____ Nightmares	_____ Overeating
_____ Work Problems	_____ Hopeless Feelings	_____ Dizziness
_____ Out of Control Behavior	_____ Sexual Difficulties	_____ Unwanted Thoughts
_____ Suicidal Thoughts	_____ Hallucinations	_____ Sporadic Dieting
_____ Blackouts/Fainting	_____ Racing Heart	_____ Stomach Problems
_____ Sleeping Too Much	_____ Apathetic	_____ Numbing Out
_____ Distrustful	_____ Buying Sprees	_____ High Risk Activities
_____ Family Arguments	_____ Often Physically Sick	_____ Hearing Voices
_____ Losing Track of Time	_____ Slowed Thinking	_____ Physical Violence
_____ Unsure of Identity	_____ Taking Pain Killers Often	

Please list the three symptoms that trouble you most:

1. _____ 2. _____ 3. _____

Day Two: A New View of Sex

Sex is…complicated. Would you agree? Whether married or single, male or female, having sex or abstaining, this three letter word has the power to evoke strong emotions and opinions in all of us. What God meant for our blessing and good has become a source of shame, pain, struggle, awkwardness and perversion. In other words, sex has become very messy. Our secret shame of sex hovers over us like a dark cloud messing with our minds, bodies, spirits and relationships. But the best thing about clouds is that when you rise above them, the sun is still shining. God's desire through this Bible study is to remove your dark "sex clouds" so you can see the sun shine bright and warm again. God's plan for sex is still good—and it can still be good for you regardless of how bad it's been in the past.

Healing for some means your once darkened sky has become clear blue, with not a cloud in sight. You'll continue to grow and learn but your healing has set you free from the shame and pain of your past. For others, the blue sky is faintly visible through a thin layer of clouds. You've had significant healing, but there is still more God wants to free you from. For others, the clouds are still dark except for that tiny, hopeful stream of light shining down on you. Yes, you are at the beginning of your healing and the end is out of sight—for now. But take heart, my friend. We all had a beginning. At least now you have *begun*.

Your view of sex has changed over the past few weeks, some more than others. Once your heart was hard toward the topic, now it's softer. For those once sickened by the thought of sex, you now see what God had always intended. Those who had no desire before, are seeing God awaken passion you never knew possible. Those who were treating it carelessly, promiscuously at the beginning of this study are discovering through new eyes-- God's eyes, how holy and precious it is. Once neglected, now it's something to cherish—and save.

Let's celebrate what God has done in you. Fill out the following with the first answers that come to your mind. In the space below, write about the feelings that you associate with sex, how you would describe sex now compared to you did at the beginning of this study.

Once again, don't spend too much time thinking about your answers. Simply write the first words that come to mind. Use present tense, as in sex is…

_____

_____

_____

_____

_____

_____

_____

Compare what you just wrote with the one you completed at the beginning of this study. How have your answers changed from the beginning? What is the most significant revelation you've had about sex during this study? To help you answer this question, spend some time reviewing your answers in Chapter Six on 'Sexual Bonding' and Chapter Ten on 'The Song of Songs'.

Thank God for the new insights He's shown you about yourself and sex over the past few weeks. Ask Him to continue to change you in this area and align your thoughts about sex with His. Write your prayer below.

Day Three: A New View of God

A lot has happened in the past twelve weeks. Relationships have been reconciled. Hearts, minds and spirits have found healing. Truth has reversed the lies. Joy has replaced shame. Victory has overcome temptation and struggle. Light reigns where once darkness prevailed. And yet in the midst of this change, one thing—one person, hasn't wavered. God. We may have changed, our lives may be different, even the people around us may seem new, but God is still who He was at the beginning of this study. If you're seeing God differently now than when you started it's not because He changed, but because you did. And now, maybe for the first time, you're seeing Him for who He really is.

- So how would you describe who God is now? How is that different from how you described Him in day one of Chapter One?

On a scale of 1-10 with 10 being the greatest, how would you rate your trust in God now? In another color pen, rate where you were trusting God at the beginning of this study.

1 _____ 10

- How has trusting God more changed your life?

On a scale of 1-10, with 10 being the greatest, how would you rate your obedience to God now? In another color pen, rate where you were obeying God at the beginning of this study.

1 _____ 10

- How has obeying God changed your life?

On a scale of 1-10, with 10 being the greatest, rate how close your relationship with God is now. With another color pen, rate where your relationship with God was at the beginning of this study.

1 _____ 10

- How has this stronger relationship with God changed your life?

- What character of God has caused the greatest source of change in you, your circumstances, or your perspective?

- What do you think changed first—your view of yourself, sex or God? How did that first change contribute to how your view of the others changed?

There are many reasons why I talked about God right at the beginning of this study. First, there would be no Bible study for sexual healing without God because I wouldn't be in the position to write one. If God hadn't pursued me and I hadn't followed Him to healing, I wouldn't have a story to share. So God is the reason I'm here—not only did He come after me, but He gave me the desire to be free from my past. Then He provided others to lead me through healing. It's His truth that set me free, His touch that made me whole. He is the one who healed me. I would still be in my prison of shame and pain today if it weren't for Him.

Second, if God created sex and all truth about sex comes from Him, then without His perspective we'd still be seeing sex our way—the wrong way. In essence, unless our perspective of who God is, changes, than nothing else in us will change.

God always has to come first. Once we discover who He is and what He wants for us in every way, including sexually, then our heart softens in response to Him and we're finally able to discern His truth. And His truth sets us free. Your perspective of yourself and sex changed because your view of God changed first. In 1 Chronicles 29, David proclaims that "everything in heaven and earth are yours, O LORD." Everything is God's, so God must come before everything.

Day Four: A New View of Others

Up until now, it's all been about you. Yes, you. Shame and pain does that. Because it's more than you can bear, you become inward focused in order to survive. There are secrets to hide, hearts to protect, reputations to maintain and shame to deny. All of this makes your self-focused energy a full time effort. There's no time to worry about how others feel. And how can you help others with their junk when you can't even face your own—let alone permit others to see it? So your shame and pain keep you isolated even when you're in a room full of friends or while serving in church with a smile.

And no one knows—at least you think they don't. If they suspect anything, it's probably just that at times you're a little self-righteous, maybe overly self-confident, a bit too controlling, a perfectionist, a little judgmental or unusually withdrawn. These are the ways I managed my pain and related to others so they wouldn't guess my shame. But it took a lot of work. And although I went through the motions at being a friend, a mom and a wife, most of my energy went to me—or more specifically, hiding the real me.

Thankfully, healing liberates us. At last we're free of our secrets, our pain, our shame and finally ourselves. No longer compelled to hide behind our 'perfect' exteriors, we're able to focus our energy and attention on others. We are free to be authentic with God, ourselves and others.

Have you begun to genuinely care about others more in the past few weeks? Has your authenticity drawn others to you like never before? Has your broken heart led to change in someone close to you? Have people been thanking you for your encouragement, your selfless love? That's what healing does to us. With the walls down, people see the real us for the first time. And guess what? They like what they see. They're drawn to us. We're no longer intimidating—we're safe. People can share their junk with us now—because they know that we *know*. Once we truly open our hearts for all to see, we are contagious. Before, our 'perfect' exterior may have impressed them, but now our life inspires them. We have just become a 'spring of living water' in a desert of lost, broken souls. If this is you, get ready because people will soon be flocking to you for a drink.

Take some time this week and ask the following people (if applicable) if they've seen a change in you since starting this study. A good question to ask is, "Do you think I've changed in the past few weeks? If so, what is different about me?" Write down what they say.

- Your husband or boyfriend:

- Your children:

- Your co-worker:

- Your friend:

- Someone you serve with at church or in your small group:

- An employer or employee:

- Parent:

- The clerk at the grocery store—just kidding...kind of:

- Your Pastor:

- Anyone else close to you I haven't mentioned:

Now we're going to repeat that same list but this time I want you to write down how *you* see *them* (or feel about them) differently since you started this study. Ask yourself this question, "How has my perception or feeling changed for this person since starting the study? What is different about how I treat them now?"

- Your husband or boyfriend:

- Your children:

- Your co-worker:

- Your friend:

- Someone you serve with at church or in your small group:

- An employer or employee:

- Parent:

- The clerk at the grocery store—this time I'm not kidding:

- Your Pastor:

- Anyone else close to you I haven't mentioned:

- Have you seen any or all of these people change in how they treat you in response to the new you? How so?

Are you surprised? Didn't realize you changed so much, right? Take a moment and bask in God's amazing grace and blessing in your life. What's He done for you that you never expected? Didn't ask for? Is beyond your wildest imagination?

Read David's prayer of praise below. Can you relate to how David feels about what God has done for him? Write out your own prayer of praise and thanks to God:

"I waited patiently for the LORD; He turned to me and heard my cry. He lifted me out of the slimy pit, out of the mud and mire; He set my feet on a rock and gave me a firm place to stand. He put a new song in my mouth, a hymn of praise to our God. Many will see and fear and put their trust in the LORD. Many O LORD, my God, are the wonders you have done. The things you planned for us no one can recount to you; were I to speak and tell of them, they would be too many to declare." (Psalm 40:1-3, 5)

Day Five: A New View of Tomorrow

Before we look at tomorrow let's stop and celebrate today. This week you've asked God to show us how He's been changing you. Whether your healing has been a lot or a little—change has happened to everyone. Don't compare yourself with anyone else—this is your journey, yours and God's. If you've poured your heart into this experience, then be confident that you are exactly where God wants you.

If your commitment to the study faltered or waned at times, and there is still some chapters or exercises left to be done—don't give up. Or if you messed up along the way—like, gave into sexual temptation, or abused your coping mechanism rather than eliminating it, don't despair. This isn't a one-time offer. God and I are not angry at you. Instead, we understand. Life happens. Sometimes the pain is just too much and we pull back. I know and it's okay. Just don't give up.

Every day is a new day—God's mercies are brand new *every* morning. Today you can start again. If you didn't finish your study, go back and complete the parts you missed. If God has revealed sin in your life, confess it to Him, accept His forgiveness and start fresh. Your journey doesn't end because the study or group does. God is with you—always. He started working on you long before you began this study, and will continue long after its done.

Either way—whether you faithfully completed every day or were hit and miss—we *all* have victories to celebrate. Yes, you too. Don't believe the enemy's lie that this has been a waste of your time or that others changed but you stayed the same, or worse—that you're such a mess you'll never be free from all your junk. None of that is true. First, God never wastes anything in our life. Secondly, we *all* change when we spend time in God's presence—we can't help it. And third, no one is too broken for God to fix. For us, yes, but with God, *nothing* is impossible.

The following questions will help you discern what God has been doing in your life during this study. Answer them prayerfully and thoughtfully—don't rush.

- One thing I can now accept which I could not accept before is:

- In the future when I am confronted with painful feelings, I will:

- I have forgiven _____ for:

- I have forgiven _____ for:

- I have forgiven _____ for:

- I have forgiven _____ for:

- I have forgiven myself for:

- I have accepted God's forgiveness for:

- I now have hope that:

- I now have joy in:

- I am grateful for:

- One way I have grown is:

- One way I can help others grow is:

- I now plan to:

Also at the beginning of this study you were asked to fill out a sheet with your goals for this study. This is what you were trusting God to do for you. Take a look at that sheet.

- Which goals were fulfilled?

- Did some of your goals change throughout the study, or did you add any new ones?

- What goals will you continue to trust God for?

- Overall, how do you feel today compared with how you felt when you started this study?

Now let's talk about the future. God works healing in our lives through many things. This study is a small part of what God is accomplishing in your life. So what does He have next for you? To help you answer these questions read the conclusion chapter in *The Invisible Bond,* called "Getting to Yes."

- What is the most significant truth you applied to your life in the course of this study?

- What area of your life experienced the most significant healing over the course of this study?

- What area of your life do you think is still in need of healing?

- What do you think is your next step in furthering your healing?

- What are you going to do to make sure you take the next step God is calling you to?

The following is a list of suggestions as you finish this study and move forward in your healing journey. Putting some of these things in place will ensure that your heart stays responsive to God's continued good work in your life.

- Be diligent about allowing God to break and humble you. Continually surrender all of yourself to Him.

- Have a regular quiet time in your sanctuary.

- Remember to take every thought captive (2 Corinthians 10:3-5).

- Review this bible study whenever you're struggling. Continue on into another group bible study. Don't isolate yourself from the body of Christ.

- Continue to evaluate your coping mechanisms and surrender them to the Lord.

- Complete your anger/forgiveness letters. Revisit this exercise of writing anger and forgiveness letters in the future when needed.

- Continue to work on your sexual history list and pray through the prayer to break bonds.

- What's your next step? There are a number of helpful studies to choose from, including: *The Wounded Heart* by Dan Allender, *Forgiven and Set Free* (a study for women seeking healing from abortion) by Linda Cochrane, Celebrate Recovery for any addictions, or any other bible study that would facilitate more healing. Some examples are: Breaking Free by Beth Moore, Search for Significance by Robert S. McGee, The Bondage Breaker by Neal T. Anderson, Healing a Father's Heart, a post-abortion bible study for men, by Linda Cochrane and Kathy Jones.

- Become a mentor for other men or women going through this study, or train to lead this study.

When you started this study on your own or in a group, you may have found it difficult or scary. If you're in a group, you didn't know each other at the beginning and may have been hesitant to share personal things about yourself. But now your group is a haven of safety and love and you don't want it to end. It's where you've experienced personal and spiritual growth. You've been fed God's truth and guided by gentle accountability. It's become a place of strength, love and hope. Now you may be afraid that when it ends you will fall back into your unhealthy, self-defeating ways.

Don't be.

There is someone who's far more invested in your healing than you are—God. He is the One who began this work in you and He has promised to keep working until you are finished—completely. Philippians 1:6 says, "*…He who began a good work in you will carry it on to completion until the day of Christ Jesus.*" God has begun a *good* work in you. And He promises to continue this good work until He's done. He doesn't say how long it will take, just that He won't stop until He's finished.

You have His eternal guarantee.

In closing, tell God how you feel about what He's done in your life during this study.

Think About It...

- What's the most significant truth you've learned this week? Write out the verse (if applicable) that God used to speak to you.

- What is God asking you to do with this new truth?

- Write out your response (prayer) to God here:

Other Books By Barbara...

THE INVISIBLE BOND
How To Break From Your Sexual Past

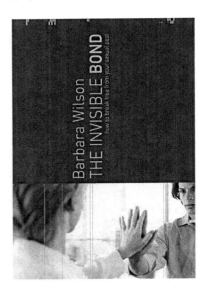

You've had sex...*But now sex has you.*

It's a past that haunts the present. Sabotaged relationships, low self-esteem, sexual dysfunction, an empty spiritual life. Sex will bind you up and tie you down. Why? It's just sex.

But "just sex" means your body, soul, mind, and spirit have become one with another. Released from a past of her own, Barbara Wilson now combines scientific research with Scripture to offer striking new insights about *what* sexual bonding is, *why* it is harmful, and *how* to move freely into your future. Complete with a study guide for group or personal use, *The Invisible Bond* is your hands-on tool for changing not your past but your *life*.

CHRISTIAN LIVING / RELATIONSHIPS / SEXUALITY
1-59052-542-6
$12.99

To order visit www.barbarawilson.org
Multnomah®
Keeping Your Trust...One Book at a Time®
www.mpbooks.com

KISS ME AGAIN
Restoring Lost Intimacy in Marriage

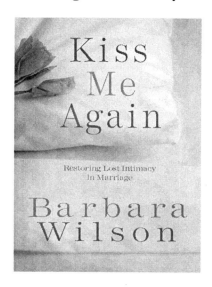

Don't let your past steal your passion.

Do you ever wonder why marriage can seem like the end of intimacy and sexual desire instead of the beginning?

Ever wonder why it was so hard to resist sex before marriage—and so easy to resist it now? If so, you're not alone! Many married women genuinely want to feel more desire toward their husbands…and can't figure out what went wrong. But there's good news. In *Kiss Me Again*, Barbara Wilson shows how powerful 'invisible bonds' from past relationships can cause heartache, disappointment, and distance for couples in the present. Then—with sensitivity, honesty, and hope—Barbara walks you step by step toward healing…and a rekindling of the closeness and passion with your husband that you really want.

You don't have to live any longer with confusion, disappointment, resentment or shame. You can rediscover desire. You can say *Wow!* again.

ISBN-13: 978-1-60142-158-6 Waterbrook Multnomah 2009.

$13.99. To order visit www.barbarawilson.org.

Assessment Forms:
[1] Adapted from *Post-Abortion Stress Symptom Checklist*, a handout used by permission from the CPC's of the Portland Metro Area. wd/heart/study/handout/post-sym/af/7-96.

Chapter Two:
[2] Michael Wells, *Problems, God's Presence, & Prayer*. Abiding Life Press, Littleton, CO. 1993. pg. 107-109.

Chapter Three:
[3] Adapted from *The Invisible Bond* © 2006 by Barbara Wilson. Used by permission of WaterBrook Multnomah Publishing Group, a division of Random House, Inc. pg. 11-12.
[4] Ibid pg. 13.
[5] Ibid, pg 117-118.
[6] John Townsend and Henry Cloud, *How People Grow*. Zondervan, Grand Rapids, MI. 2001. pg. 215.
[7] Adapted from *The Invisible Bond* © 2006 by Barbara Wilson. Used by permission of WaterBrook Multnomah Publishing Group, a division of Random House, Inc. pg. 89-90.

Chapter Four:
[8] Linda Dillow and Lorraine Pintus, *Intimate Issues*. Waterbrook, Colorado Springs, CO. 1999. pg. 199-201.
[9] Shannon Ethridge, *Every Women's Battle*. Waterbrook, Colorado Springs, CO. 2003. pg. 39-43.
[10] Ibid, pg. 75.
[11] Henry Blackaby, *Experiencing God*. LifeWay Press, Nashville, TN. 1990. pg. 20.

Chapter Five:
[12] Dan Allender. *The Wounded Heart*. Navpress, Colorado Springs, CO> 1990. pg. 26
[13] Ibid, pg. 26
[14] Ibid pg. 192.
[15] Ibid pg. 25.
[16] Charles Price, *Stop Trying To Live For Jesus…Let Him Live Through You*. Kingsway Publications, Eastborne, England. 1995. pg. 155.
[17] Ibid pg. 156-157.

Chapter Six:
[18] Linda Dillow and Lorraine Pintus, *Intimate Issues*. Waterbrook, Colorado Springs, CO. 1999. pg. 6-9.
[19] Randy Alcorn, *Restoring Sexual Sanity*. Coral Ridge Ministries, Ft. Lauderdale, FL. 2000. pg. 120.
[20] Ibid, pg. 120.

Chapter Seven:
[21] Anger Questionnaire adapted from anonymous (unidentified) handout.

Chapter Nine:
[22] Adapted from *The Invisible Bond* © 2006 by Barbara Wilson. Used by permission of WaterBrook Multnomah Publishing Group, a division of Random House, Inc. pg. 108.
[23] Ibid pg. 110.
[24] Neil T. Anderson, *The Bondage Breaker*. Harvest House Publishers, Eugene, Oregon. 2000. pg. 223 (some – not all--of the points are from this book).

Chapter Ten:
[25] Linda Dillow and Lorraine Pintus, *Intimate Issues*. Waterbrook, Colorado Springs, CO. 1999. pg. 18.
Chapter Eleven:

[26] Adapted from a handout by Nancy Leigh DeMoss, 'Proud People vs Broken People. Find Nancy at Revive Our Hearts, www.reviveourhearts.com.

[27] Rick Warren, *The Purpose Driven Life*. Zondervan, Grand Rapids, MI. 2002. pg. 246-247.

[28] Adapted from *Breaking Sexual Ties,* a handout created by Kathy Edwards, copied by permission, we\allheart\hrt-study\handouts\sexties.doc\03-96\af

Chapter Twelve:

[29] Who I Am in Christ handout

[30] Adapted from *Post-Abortion Stress Symptom Checklist,* a handout used by permission from the CPC's of the Portland Metro Area. wd/heart/study/handout/post-sym/af/7-96.